Cooking with Berries

Cooking with Berries

BY MARGARET WOOLFOLK

Clarkson N. Potter, Inc./Publishers NEW YORK
DISTRIBUTED BY CROWN PUBLISHERS INC.

Inquiries should be addressed to
Clarkson N. Potter, Inc.,
One Park Avenue,
New York, N.Y. 10016

Printed in the United States of America

Published simultaneously in Canada by
General Publishing Company Limited

Library of Congress Cataloging in Publication Data
Main entry under title:

Cooking with berries.

Includes index.
1. Cookery (Berries) 2. Berries. I. Woolfolk, Margaret.
TX813.B4C66   641.6'6'47   78-31279
ISBN 0-517-53429-0
ISBN 0-517-53716-8 pbk.

 CONTENTS

For Mandy, Lisa, and Jenny—
with the hope that they will always
enjoy warm days in the sun

Chapter One
The Art of Picking Berries

$\mathcal{A}$ sun-drenched field. The humming of locusts. And a thicket ripe with berries!

Such an idyllic setting recalls other such scenes that transcend the centuries and provide an unconscious link with our ancestors who searched for and used Nature's food. Long after maturity is reached, a man will fondly recount his youthful berrying expeditions into the countryside and the special foods that were made with the harvest. The primitive act of picking berries is a warm, peaceful experience that offers assurance of the continuity of the ages.

The act itself has no mystique about it—it doesn't require fashionable clothing, can be done alone or collectively by young and old, and its cost ranges from nothing to little. It has the suspense of an Easter egg hunt—for you never know what you will discover. It offers the tranquil therapy of a day in the sun and it is an opportunity to reach out and literally touch nature with all the senses. Finally, of course, it provides the harvester with food that can be savored warm from the bush or prepared as a gourmet's exotic delight.

Like most human endeavors—even the simplest—berrying requires a finesse, or art, based partly on common sense, partly on knowledge, and wholly on good manners.

1

Choosing the best time of day to go berrying can present something of a problem. Because berries will readily spoil when wet, it is necessary to pick them after the sun has burned the dew off the fruit. If you wait until afternoon, the heat of the day can be uncomfortable, while evening picking is usually done in the company of buzzing mosquitoes. The ideal time—if it is possible to arrange—is around midmorning when it is still relatively cool. This has the added advantage of giving you the rest of the day to begin processing the harvest rather than trying to store it all in the refrigerator until the next day.

The time of day and the type of berry you are picking will dictate what clothing to wear. Obviously, you do not want to ruin your best tennis whites, so think in terms of gardening clothes that will not be affected by a few stains of ripe berry juice. Since many wild berries prefer the damp soil that mosquitoes call home, you may want to cover your arms with a protecting shirt. Shorts, although cool and comfortable, make you vulnerable to bug bites and torn skin.

When you find an abundant patch of berries, try to resist the "squirrel instinct" to take home everything. Because the fruit is so perishable, it is wasteful to pick more than you can readily use or process. Rather than have the fruit spoil, leave the excess on the bush for others to pick, or for the birds to enjoy. Incidentally, the birds will repay your kindness by scattering the seeds as they eat, which will result in new berry patches in future years. The unripe fruit—left on the bush to mature—will also provide you with another chance to pick the following week.

Because damaged bushes will not bear large crops in the following years, it is important to be careful as you harvest the yield. Try not to trample and break the canes and branches as you stretch to reach that "one perfect berry," for it may cost you some of next year's crop. Children, especially, need to be reminded of this as their enthusiasm sends them darting into bushes.

Children are wonderful berry pickers and help to fill the family pails quickly. They have a feeling of contributing to the family welfare when they proudly show how much they have picked. In our family each child carries her own pail and decides what it is she wants made from the fruit. Whether it is jam or a favorite bread, the child helps with the preparation and serves it at a future meal. Children, because of their height, have the advantage of being able to see berries that are overlooked by adults. Blackberries, for example, not only have fruit on the tops of the thicket but produce many berries that are hidden beneath the covering leaves. Our youngest— and shortest—child picks large quantities of berries because she looks up and under the areas that adults have thought to be harvested completely.

If, in your search of the countryside for berries, you find a patch that is on land that is obviously owned and used, ask permission before you begin to fill your pails. The farmer, or his children, may have plans to use that fruit. Berries are often earmarked for picking by the youngsters in the family to be sold at a roadside stand. If, however, the landowner invites you to help yourself, it is a thoughtful and appreciated gesture to return the next day with a berry pie or jar of jam as a thank you. This consideration is not only polite but guaranteed to make the generous neighbor more receptive next year when you would again like to pick berries.

An obvious warning, but one that needs to be repeated, is to *know* any berry before you pick and eat it. If you are unsure of the identification, leave it. The State Agricultural Department of your area will identify any unknown berry when you send a sample of the fruit and leaves of the plant. The local college or high-school botany department may also be able to provide assistance in identifying any unusual species that you find.

Finally, and most importantly, the true art of berry picking is to *enjoy* it! It is a fun experience—despite the sometimes sweltering temperatures, pesky mosquitoes, and painful thorns. When you return home you will discover that you have gotten more from your expedition than a pail of sun-warmed berries. You will have participated in the annual cycle of fruition and harvesting that has sustained life through the ages. It is a celebration of summer!

Chapter Two
Making the Most of Berries

Berries, like most fruits and vegetables, ripen within a short span of several weeks and are then gone for another year. Unlike some of the other seasonal bounty, berries can be successfully used in such a variety of ways that the "taste of summer" can be savored throughout the year. In addition to canning and freezing the fresh fruit, berries can be made into jams and jellies, wine, cordial, and ice cream—to be stored and enjoyed at another time.

Aside from being fun, finding and using the "free food" available is a practical economic boost to every homemaker's budget. Commercial berry products—such as jam and frozen pies—are usually high-priced luxury items. By providing your own labor in gathering and preparing the fruit these luxuries can be a regular part of your menu planning.

These various methods of food preparation not only give you the pleasure of gourmet delicacies, but by using your imagination—and the recipes in this collection—you can have a wide selection of conserves, chutneys, wines, and breads unavailable at any price. Whether it is Spiced Fresh Currants (page 129), Cranberry Chutney (page 104), or Raspberry-Cherry Conserve (page 163), you will enjoy the taste of something different that can turn an ordinary supper into an adventure.

After the initial work of processing the berries, the foods you have stored in your pantry and freezer are a convenience that result in appetizing, easily prepared meals throughout the year. Breads, cakes, and pies—made during the berry season and stored in the freezer—will often be the perfect addition to a quick family supper when you are running late. Chicken quickly becomes an exotic Oriental dish with the addition of Spiced Blackberry Relish (page 42) and orange slices. Even gift giving is helped with the convenience of a fully stocked pantry. The colorful jars of jams and relishes are always there for a last minute hostess gift or something special for a shut-in. And during the holidays your originality and thoughtfulness will be appreciated by friends who enjoy good food.

By using basic kitchen methods you and your family will harvest the rewards of berrying long after summer ends and the locusts stop humming.

FREEZING BERRIES

Owning and efficiently using a freezer is one of the homemaker's greatest aids in menu planning. My own "squirrel instincts" are satisfied whenever I open the freezer door and see stacks of neatly packaged and labeled vegetables, fruits, pies, ice cream, and breads. Because of the relative ease with which food may be prepared for freezer storage, it is possible to harvest and save large quantities of berries.

Berries need to be frozen at their peak of ripeness and flavor in airtight, leakproof containers. Always label and date the packages and plan to store them no longer than nine or ten months.

After sorting, washing in cold water, and draining the berries, they may be prepared for the freezer in one of three ways. The dry, unsweetened pack is quickly accomplished by spreading the berries on cookie sheets and storing in the freezer for three to four hours, or until the fruit is hard. The berries can then be put in heavy plastic bags or polyethylene boxes. This dry-pack method is especially successful if the berries are to be used for pies or jam at a later date. The advantage of this method is that the berries are individually frozen, which allows you to remove a handful of fruit from the package when you are preparing muffins or pancakes.

The sugar-syrup pack is the preferred method for fruit that is to be served uncooked—such as whole blueberries that you might serve on pudding. The syrup is made by boiling two to three cups of sugar—depending on your own preference for sweetness—in one quart of water. When the sugar is dissolved, allow the mixture to cool before filling the quart-size freezer container one-third full with the liquid. Add the cleaned berries to the container, being sure to leave a one-inch head space for expansion.

The third method of freezing berries, and the one that seems most satisfactory with strawberries, is the sugar pack. Spread one quart of berries (if doing strawberries, slice them first) in a shallow pan and sprinkle with three-quarters cup of sugar. With a spatula, carefully stir the berries until the fruit is coated. Immediately pack the berries into containers, leaving one-half to an inch head space, and freeze before the sugar draws juices from the fruit.

The method you select for freezing berries is determined by the berry you are working with and its intended use. In all cases the amount of sugar you add should be adjusted to accommodate the natural sweetness of the fruit and your own taste, so don't be afraid to experiment with the sweetening.

The following chart lists the berries and the freezing methods that can be used with each.

| Blackberries and Dewberries | Dry Pack
Sugar Syrup Pack
Sugar Pack |

Blueberries and Elderberries	Dry Pack Sugar Syrup Pack Sugar Pack
Cranberries	Dry Pack
Currants	Dry Pack Sugar Syrup Pack (crush fruit slightly) Sugar Pack
Gooseberries	Dry Pack
Raspberries	Sugar Syrup Pack Sugar Pack
Strawberries (slice strawberries for freezing)	Sugar Syrup Pack Sugar Pack

CANNING BERRIES

There was a time when canning was the main method by which homemakers could preserve the summer harvests for winter use. Home freezers have given us another, and sometimes easier, way of storing food but canning is still an economical and practical convenience. Freezers—as wonderful as they are—provide a limited amount of storage space. In an abundant year, when generous friends share their garden bounty with you or the local orchards hang heavy with inexpensive fruit, a combination of freezing and canning will provide the most efficient means of saving food.

The colorful jars—labeled and lined up on pantry shelves—will keep flavor and nutritional value for a long time while helping to answer the question—"What's for supper?"

The same process that puts canned fruits and vegetables on your supermarket shelves can be accomplished at home on a smaller scale. Canning, or bottling, summer fruits is a method of storing food in syrup in jars that have been vacuum sealed. The vacuum seal, essential in preventing bacteria from contaminating the food, is achieved by heating the jars immediately after they are packed with the fruit and syrup.

The heating of packed jars is referred to as a boiling water bath and is done in a water-bath canner—a large kettle with a cover and inside rack that prevents the jars from resting directly on the bottom of the kettle. Because the packed jars must be completely covered by boiling water, it is necessary for the kettle to be deep enough to cover the tops of the jars and to allow the water to boil. This canner, although a specialized piece of equipment, will more than pay for itself by enabling you to save money at the grocery store. Most kitchen supply shops or hardware stores carry a complete line of canning equipment during the summer months when people are harvesting their gardens.

The seal of a processed jar (a jar that has been processed in the boiling water bath) can be tested by pressing down the center of the lid with your finger. If there is a depression in the center of the lid—and it stays down when pressed—the jar is sealed and can be safely stored for a year. Although the food may be eaten after a year, there is some loss of color and flavor after that time. For efficiency, most homemakers try to estimate their food needs and can only what will be used before the next harvesting season.

General Instructions
1. Fill water-bath canner with enough hot water to cover the jars you will use. Place canner on stove to heat.

2. Check jars for flaws. Discard any with nicks or cracks on sealing surfaces. Wash in hot, sudsy water and rinse. Leave jars in scalding water until ready to use.

3. Wash and drain firm, ripe fruit in ice water.

4. Prepare fruit according to the instructions, given below, for either the cold or the hot-pack method, doing only enough for one canner load at a time.

5. When fruit is packed in jars with syrup (see below), remove air bubbles by gently working a table knife down the

sides of the jar. If necessary, add more liquid to cover fruit, but *always* leave a half-inch head space.

6. To ensure a good seal, wipe top and threads with a clean, damp cloth to remove any food particles.

7. Adjust lids on jars according to manufacturer's directions.

8. Lower prepared jars into hot—not boiling—water in canner, being sure jars do not touch. Jars must be completely covered by water.

9. Bring water to a boil and reduce heat to maintain a steady but gentle boil. Processing time begins when the water reaches a rolling boil.

10. Remove jars at end of processing and cool upright on cloths, away from draft.

11. Test jars for seal when cold (see below). Refrigerate and quickly use contents of any jar that did not seal, or reprocess contents in a clean, scalded jar with new lid.

12. Wipe sealed jars with a damp cloth and label and date before storing in a cool, dark, dry place.

When canning berries, the fruit is packed in a light or medium syrup, depending on your preference. Light syrup is made by combining two cups of sugar with one quart of water or fruit juice in a medium saucepan. Cook the mixture until the sugar dissolves for about five minutes. Keep the mixture hot until ready to pour into packed jars. Medium syrup is prepared in the same way as light but has a higher sugar content, using three cups of sugar with one quart of water.

Except for strawberries, which lose flavor and color when canned, all berries may be successfully preserved by some method of canning. The soft berries that do not hold their shape well—blackberries, dewberries, raspberries, and mulberries—require a raw (cold) pack. After washing one to two quarts of berries in ice water, stem and drain the fruit. Pour half a cup of light or medium syrup into the hot, empty jar. Pack the raw, cold berries into the jar, shaking the container down to pack the fruit tightly without crushing. Leaving a half-inch head space, add more hot syrup, if necessary, to completely cover the fruit. Adjust the cap and process in a boiling water bath—15 minutes for pints, 20 minutes for quarts.

The hot-pack method is used with firm berries such as blueberries, currants, elderberries, and gooseberries. After washing and draining the berries, put them in a large kettle. For each quart of berries, add one-quarter to one-half cup of sugar and allow the mixture to stand for one hour. Cover the kettle and heat—shaking the pan occasionally to prevent sticking—until sugar is dissolved and berries are boiling hot. Pour the hot fruit and juice into hot, sterilized jars, leaving a half-inch head space. Adjust lids and process in a boiling water bath—ten minutes for pints, fifteen minutes for quarts.

Cranberries—the Thanksgiving favorite—are the exception to the raw-pack and hot-pack methods described here. Other than freezing the whole berries, the way to "put up" cranberries is by preparing the traditional sauce, as explained in a later chapter.

By always using berries at their peak of flavor and following the instructions for their processing, your "berry season" can extend throughout the year. The effort involved in "putting up" fresh fruit not only saves money and time but adds summer variety to winter eating.

Equipment for Canning

Colander

Widemouthed canning funnel (optional)

Glass canning jars—quarts and pints

Two-piece metal caps with self-sealing lids

Water-bath canner

For a complete handbook of canning information, send $1.00 for the *Ball Blue Book* to Ball Corporation, Muncie, Indiana 47302.

A hot summer day and people are gathered on the porch. The center of attention is an ice-cream freezer and the rhythmic squeak of the crank as it slowly, and then rapidly, churns the fruit and cream into a thick froth of flavor.

Although this vision of summer activity is more associated with the Victorian era and gingerbread houses than it is with contemporary life, families are increasingly discovering the pleasures—and economical advantages—of simple, old-fashioned fun.

Despite the laborsaving benefits of electric ice-cream makers, we still prefer our hand-cranked freezer. It not only produces a finer textured ice cream but it evokes fond childhood memories for any adults who happen to be visiting at the time. Old family recipes and stories of ice-cream making are invariably exchanged, while children beg to lick the dasher.

When planning to make churn-frozen ice creams, prepare and chill the mixture six to twelve hours in advance. This allows the flavors to blend and helps to produce a smoother ice cream. When ready, fill the can of the freezer three-quarters full, adjust the dasher in place, and cover. Pack crushed ice around the bottom third of the can and then layer rock salt and ice until the freezer is full. Use four to six quarts of ice to one cup of rock salt, adding more as melting occurs. Turn the crank slowly at first, increasing speed as the mixture thickens and expands. If the ice cream is to be served at once—and few friends will want to wait for their reward—it should be frozen harder than if you plan to save it in the home freezer.

Although few people think of ice cream as a way of preserving fruits and berries, it is possible to store this classic dessert for six weeks in the freezer without loss of flavor or quality. Pack it in airtight containers, leaving a half-inch head space, and store it in the coldest part of the freezer. To prevent ice crystals from forming, place a piece of wax paper or plastic wrap, cut to fit, over the mixture before securing the cover.

Because the storage time for ice cream is relatively short, we make only the amount that will be eaten within that time. By using some of our frozen berries to make ice cream throughout the year, we are able to enjoy the summer-fresh flavors without regard for the season.

MAKING JAMS AND JELLIES

At our house the Christmas celebration really begins in June with the ripening and picking of the first berries. It is then that I plan the assortment of conserves, spiced jams, marmalades, and jellies to be made during the summer months to be given as holiday gifts. As each berry comes into season, the house is filled with tempting aromas while jewellike jars of red, gold, and deep blue begin to fill the pantry. When the holiday finally arrives, festive bows decorate baskets of gourmet delights to be given to neighbors, friends, and elderly acquaintances who might otherwise not receive many surprises during the Yuletide season.

Jams and jellies are the delicious blending of fruit, sugar, pectin, and acid. All fruits have some natural pectin and acid—which are crucial to the jellying process—but the amount can vary considerably with the year, the soil, and the area where you live. Because of these uncertainties, which can result in too many jars of berry sauce, I prefer to add commercial liquid pectin to many of my fruit spreads. In the recipes in this collection where no pectin is added, the fruits have a high enough level of natural pectin to assure good results. Lemon juice, added to the cooking fruit, is the necessary acid. The final product is a firm, flavorful spread that can be stored for one to two years.

When preparing any type of jam or jelly, it is advisable to cook only small amounts of fruit at one time. To obtain the best flavor, the fruit mixtures should be cooked quickly until they reach the thickened stage. Because doubled quantities require longer cooking, the final product is less flavorful.

As with any method of preserving, use fresh fruits at their peak of flavor—unless a recipe specifically requires underripe fruit. Because underripe fruit is usually sour, the sweetness of the jam or jelly will be affected by using anything less than mature berries. Making jam and jelly is an exact science that demands that you follow the recipes as they are given. Aside from adding spices or citrus peel for a different flavor, this is not the place to experiment without risking the entire batch of jam or jelly.

When preparing to make jam or jelly, assemble the necessary equipment before you actually begin. This organization not only makes the work easier but saves time at the crucial stages of packing and sealing the jars. Thoroughly wash and drain the fruit in a colander—discarding any imperfect berries. Use a large cooking pot of stainless steel or unchipped enamel and never fill it more than two-thirds full—to allow for the bubbles and foam that are produced with a rolling boil. If the fruit is being made into jelly, it is necessary to strain the juice from the berries after they have cooked according to the recipe. By using a jelly bag (or four thicknesses of muslin) it is possible to obtain a clear, bright fruit juice that results in a clear jelly product. For ease of packing the jars, I prefer to use a widemouthed canning funnel that prevents the dripping of hot, sticky jam over hands, countertop, and the outside of the jars. However, heavy-duty foil can be shaped into a widemouthed rim to serve this purpose.

Once the jars are packed with jam or jelly, it is necessary to make the jars airtight so that bacteria cannot contaminate the food. Two-piece metal caps with self-sealing lids are available—with instructions for use—at most supermarkets and many hardware stores. These lids seal automatically as the contents of the jars cool and form an airtight vacuum.

A less expensive method of sealing jams and jellies—but one that involves a little more work—is to cover the fruit spread with a layer of melted paraffin. Never try to melt paraffin over direct heat as it will spatter and smoke. To spare myself the clean-up job of removing hardened paraffin from the top of a double boiler, I place the new bars of paraffin in a disposable aluminum pie plate and set it over a pan of boiling water. The layer of wax must be a quarter to a third of an inch thick and completely cover the surface of the contents. After the paraffin has cooled and hardened, the jars may be further sealed with caps or foil that is secured with twine.

Finally, store the jars in a dark, relatively cool area of the house. Then, on a snowy January morning, when you are wondering why you got out of bed, open that special storage place and select something to brighten breakfast. With the distinctive addition of Apricot-Blackcap Marmalade (page 166), Spiced Elderberry Jam (page 205), or a unique berry combination of your own, an ordinary morning meal can be as charming and refreshing as a visit to an old country inn.

Equipment for Making Jams, Jellies, and Conserves

Colander

Large wide cooking pot of stainless steel or unchipped enamel

Jelly bag (or four thicknesses of muslin) for straining juice from fruit in jelly making

Widemouthed canning funnel (optional)

Glass fruit jars

Two-piece metal caps with self-sealing lids or bars of paraffin to be melted for sealing fruit spreads

Although the origin of wine is somewhat obscure, it is felt by historians that fermented fruit beverages were known—albeit accidentally—by primitive man. Our first personal experience with wine making was probably similar to that of a surprised caveman thousands of years earlier. After picking and processing several gallons of blackberries one day, I absentmindedly left the remaining gallon of fruit on the counter when I turned off the lights and went to bed. The following morning I noticed a peculiar odor that became stronger as I approached the kitchen. It didn't take long to discover the source of the aroma! The perfectly ripe berries—in the darkness and summer heat of the kitchen—had begun the natural process of fermentation. Unwilling to lose the gallon of berries, we did some quick research about wine making and added the necessary sugar and water to our brew. The resulting wine, when tasted months later, was not the most delicate wine we have ever had, but it was quite palatable and added a nice flavor to cooked dishes. Since that time we have broadened our knowledge and refined our techniques of wine making to the point where we produce a wide variety of fruit and berry wines to be enjoyed at home and given as gifts.

Wine is basically the blending of fruit, sugar, and yeast in the proper quantities. The sugar is changed into alcohol by fermentation that is performed by the yeast. Some fruits—such as grapes and currants—have natural wine yeast growing on the skins, but with most fruits it is necessary to add a wine yeast that is available at a wine-making supply store. Contrary to the recommendations of some books on the subject, baker's yeast is not a substitute for wine yeast—although it will produce fermentation.

As with making jams and jellies, cleanliness of equipment is an important factor in the success of your efforts. The storage and wine bottles should be thoroughly washed and then heated in a 250 °F oven for fifteen minutes. The other equipment (rubber tubing, spatula, and ceramic crock) can be made relatively germ-free by soaking in scalding water. These precautions, although time consuming, will help you to produce a good wine.

When you first begin making wine at home, it is possible to work with a small amount of basic, inexpensive equipment. The fermenting container—a wide-mouthed, two-gallon vessel—can be a ceramic crock or a plastic pail, available at any department or hardware store. The berries, sugar, water, and yeast are combined in this container and covered with plastic wrap to ferment, in the dark, at room temperature. A dark closet is a safe storage place during this period. As the fermentation occurs, bubbles and foam rise to the surface of the mixture and need to be pushed down twice daily with an ordinary kitchen spatula or wooden spoon.

At the end of this violent fermentation period—which lasts from four to seven days, depending on the type of fruit and the recipe you are using—it is necessary to strain the juice from the fruit. As when making jelly, the object is to get as clear a fruit liquid as possible and a jelly bag is a convenient piece of equipment for accomplishing this. Four thicknesses of muslin or a closely woven dish towel can serve the same purpose.

The strained juice is then transferred to a clean one-gallon glass jug for the second phase of fermentation. This is a gradual, slower process of fermentation that lasts from three to four weeks, during which time the alcohol content is increasing. When the jug is filled with the strained liquid—leaving a four-inch head space—the mouth of the container is sealed with a fermentation lock, a device that allows for the escape of carbon dioxide while preventing air from reaching the wine. These locks (also known as water seals) are available inexpensively at wine-making supply shops.

Throughout this time of fermentation and the following storage period, deposits of dead yeast and particles of fruit—called *lees*—will settle to the bottom of the container. By periodically siphoning the wine with a three-foot length of plastic tubing from one container to another (racking), you can easily separate out this unwanted material. These rackings are important to the quality of the final product because the lees may impart an off-taste to the wine and make it cloudy. If solid particles continue to cloud the wine after repeated rackings, you may stir in some leaf gelatin (available from a pharmacist) at the third racking to help clear the liquid. Cloudiness can also be the result of natural pectin in the fruit. If you are making wine from fruit which is high in pectin—such as raspberries—you should add a pectic enzyme.

The final stage of wine making, and perhaps the most satisfying, is the bottling. Although it is possible to purchase new wine bottles, we have always used the ones empty of commercial wine. Once your friends know what you are doing, you will probably receive more donated bottles than you will be able to fill. It is necessary, however, always to use new corks, which can be purchased at a wine-making supply store, along with a small, inexpensive corking device.

While browsing through the fascinating shops that cater to home vintners, treat yourself to some of the attractive labels that add a professional touch to your efforts. They will not only look handsome but will help with the necessary record keeping of wine making. Because the wines are made at different times and require varying periods of aging, it is important to mark the bottles and keep a small notebook of pertinent information.

Several years ago, after reading about a wine auction where century-old bottles of currant wine were appreciatively opened, we decided to make some currant wine. After the necessary aging period, we sampled one bottle and found it to be delicious. The following year, and every year since, we have opened another bottle of the same wine and discovered that it was even better than the previous year's sample. We now have only three bottles of that particular vintage left and we will not be sampling them for some time because we are saving one for each of our children. On some grand occasion that we are not even aware of yet, we will open a bottle in celebration and tell the story of how we made the wine when they were babies. I doubt that our currant wine will reach the century mark but we will look forward with anticipation to a fine toast with our homemade wine.

Basic Wine-Making Equipment *

1 3-gallon plastic bucket
1 3-gallon ceramic crock (or plastic pail)
2 1-gallon glass jugs
   Spatula (for pressing down fruit cap)
   Fermentation locks
   Wine bottles
   Plastic tubing—3 feet long (for siphoning)
   Pectic enzyme
   Campden tablets
   Dry packaged wine yeast
   Plastic wrap
   Hand corker
   Corks
   Labels

* Avoid using metal utensils unless they are enameled and use only equipment that has *not* been in contact with vinegar.

Chapter Three
The Bramble Berries

Blackberries, one of the most abundant of wild fruits, have been known throughout the temperate regions of the world for centuries. It is believed that blackberry brambles formed the crown of thorns worn by Christ as well as the burning bush in which the Lord appeared to Moses. These associations may have fostered the myth that the devil hates blackberries and withers the bushes wherever he can by throwing his cloak over them.

Blackberry picking has always had a special significance for our family because of an old English fairy tale associated with the fruit. Our identical twin girls have delighted in the retelling of the story of twin sisters—Princess Olwen, fair and gentle, and Princess Gertha, mean and bitter. At the urging of the foul-tempered sister, the father of the girls commanded a witch to "put the form of a bramble on Olwen forever . . . and make her fruit green and black by turns, and sour, and the stems thorny." Although they would deny it, I am sure our twins have occasionally thought there would be merit to such a curse—provided it was the other twin who was affected!

The story continues when a prince, loving the fair maiden, employs the white magic of the court wizard to transform himself into a bird so he can fly to the disguised princess and pluck the ripest berry of the bramble bush. The prince carries it to the wizard, who undoes the spell and restores Olwen to her natural form. Everyone, as they must in fairy tales, lives happily ever after and our playful discussions of this story—while harvesting the plump, ripe berries—make outings amid the brambles a special time of family fun.

Historically, blackberries have been considered to be a good remedy for various ailments in addition to possessing a sweet and refreshing flavor. While there is no scientific evidence to support this belief in the medicinal qualities of blackberries, it is known that they do have a higher level of vitamin B_1 and calcium than other fruits. Country doctors of long ago were often judged on the merits of their blackberry "tonic." An old mountain recipe—a favorite of elderly ladies—called for the boiling of one pound of sugar with a pint of water until fairly thick. One pint of ripe berry juice and half a grated nutmeg were then added to the syrup and boiled for fifteen minutes. The recipe was completed with the addition of a half pint of brandy, after which the "medicine" was bottled. The dosage—for summer complaint, dizziness, chills, or whatever—usually suggested one tablespoon for a child and half a glass for an adult. Although blackberry "tonic" is no longer dispensed by doctors, many people still consider Blackberry Wine (page 43) to be a delicious and effective curative.

Wild blackberry bushes are readily found along the hedgerows of the countryside and bordering wooded areas throughout the Northern Hemisphere. The canes grow from three to nine feet high and are often recognized by their distinctive arch. The location of the thickets should be noted by the prospective berry picker in mid-spring before surrounding foliage obscures the brambles. Because the wild canes multiply and spread so thickly, they provide safe refuge for birds and other small wildlife that compete with the berry pickers at harvesttime.

The brambles do not surrender their plump, juicy fruit easily. Curved thorns that cover the canes will snare the clothes and ankles of the careless harvester. But blackberries are well worth the struggle for they are the largest of the wild berries, and will fill the buckets quickly. Because the core, which clings to the fruit, is hard and distasteful in the underripe berry, blackberries must be picked and used when they are perfectly ripe. Ruby red when unripe, they turn purplish blue black as they mature and are from half an inch to an inch long. Although their thimblelike shape might mislead one into thinking they are thimbleberries, the blackberry is always identifiable by the center core to which the numerous drupelets cling.

Because blackberries thrive in the wild, they are one of the easiest fruits for the home gardener to cultivate. They are best planted in rich soil during the early spring. A heavy layer of mulch—decaying leaves work well—helps to retain moisture, which is especially necessary in midsummer. The harvest from plants in dry soil tends to be small and less flavorful. If the bushes are compatible with the soil, they will flourish and multiply too rapidly unless pruned. The established plants should be cut back to fifteen inches every spring to maintain strong new growth and to ensure a plentiful harvest in July or August.

A near relative of the blackberry that we first discovered while walking a sandy path in Cape Cod is the dewberry. The trailing stems of the plants lie on the ground, providing excellent cover for ground-nesting birds. The fruit is not as shiny, nor as large as the blackberry, but has a delicate flavor and ripens earlier than its cane counterpart. Dewberries grow successfully in dry or stony soil and are found along roadways and railroad tracks throughout the United States. Substitution of dewberries for blackberries usually brings good results in cooking and few people can distinguish between blackberry pie and dewberry pie—especially when it is savored warm from the oven.

The loganberry, similar in appearance to the blackberry, is a variety of red dewberry. Found in warmer climates, it is primarily used for commercial canning. Loganberry jam is a special breakfast treat during the winter months, and if one has the patience to wait two years for the harsh taste to disappear, it is possible to produce a good table wine from loganberries.

When picking berries, as when buying, you should select plump, ripe berries with good color. Because damp berries will mold quickly, it is best to arrange your picking time late enough in the day to allow the sun to burn the dew off the fruit. Blackberries can be easily frozen if you harvest more than you can immediately use. Spread the unwashed fruit—separated—on cookie sheets and store in the freezer for three to four hours. When hard, the berries may be put in airtight containers or special plastic bags. The frozen fruit can then be used to turn a winter meal into a summer celebration when added to pancakes, pies, or cobblers.

Spiced Blackberry Compote

 Fresh fruits—simply prepared—are a good prelude to the entrée.

¼ cup sugar
½ cup water
½ teaspoon fresh lime
   juice
1 2-inch stick
   cinnamon

3 whole cloves
   dash of salt
2 cups fresh
   blackberries,
   washed

Boil together all the ingredients except the blackberries in a small saucepan for 3 to 4 minutes. Cool and remove cinnamon stick and cloves. Pour the mixture over the blackberries and refrigerate, stirring occasionally, for several hours. Serve the compote in long-stemmed glasses.

Yield: 4 servings.

Black and White Appetizer

An elegant, easily prepared appetizer that I used to save for formal dinner parties. By arranging the fruit in one large serving dish, however, it becomes a delicious accompaniment to an informal supper of cold pork or fowl.

3 cups seedless green grapes

3 cups fresh blackberries

¾ cup honey

¾ cup cognac

1 tablespoon lemon juice

1½ cups sour cream

Thoroughly wash and drain the grapes and blackberries, removing any stems. Combine honey, cognac, and lemon juice. Gently toss the fruit in the honey mixture. Let stand in refrigerator for 5 to 6 hours, stirring occasionally. Mound in chilled, stemmed glasses and top with sour cream just before serving.

Yield: 6 servings.

Blackberry Soup

 The best time to serve any fruit soup is at lunch on a very hot day. For added appeal, accompany this soup with plates of fresh pineapple sticks and fruit fritters, which are fried, batter-dipped fruit slices.

2 cups blackberries, washed	2 cloves
1 small lemon, thinly sliced	½ cup sugar
2 cups cold water	¼ cup orange juice
1 1-inch stick cinnamon	2 cups sour cream
	lemon slices (garnish)

Place all ingredients, except sour cream and the garnish, in a saucepan and bring the mixture to a boil. Lower the heat and simmer gently for 10 minutes, or until the berries are soft. Work the soup through a fine sieve and refrigerate for 3 hours. Blend in the sour cream just before serving and garnish with lemon slices.

Yield: 4 servings.

Summer Celebration Salad

 Fruits in this salad may be varied according to whim or availability. Perfect for a patio party!

1 large watermelon	1 quart fresh strawberries, washed and hulled
1 large pineapple, peeled, cored, and cubed	1 quart fresh blackberries, washed
1 cantaloupe, seeded and cut into balls	1 quart sweet cherries, pitted
1 honeydew melon, seeded and cut into balls	2 bananas, peeled and sliced

Place the watermelon on its side and carefully slice off the top third of the melon. Scoop meat out of the shell, discarding the seeds. Drain liquid. With a sharp knife, cut the rim of the large shell in scallop fashion. Cut watermelon meat into bite-sized pieces. Prepare other fruits and place them in melon bowl. Toss gently to mix. Chill. Just before serving, toss fruit with Celebration Dressing.

Celebration Dressing

2 teaspoons soy sauce	¼ cup orange juice concentrate
½ teaspoon Tabasco sauce	¼ cup honey
2 tablespoons lime juice	1 cup mayonnaise
	1 cup sour cream
	grated rind of 1 lime

Combine soy sauce, Tabasco, lime juice, orange juice concentrate, and honey. Blend mixture into mayonnaise. Stir in sour cream and grated lime. Add to Summer Celebration Salad and toss well.

Yield: 15 to 20 servings.

Cantaloupe and Blackberry Salad

This salad is good enough to be a luncheon entrée with cheese popovers or brown bread.

salad greens
1 ripe cantaloupe, chilled
2 cups fresh blackberries, washed
¼ cup toasted almonds, slivered

Arrange the salad greens on four individual salad plates. Halve and seed the cantaloupe, cutting two rings from each side. Peel the rings and place on greens. Make balls from remaining cantaloupe and mix gently with blackberries and almonds. Place the mixture on the melon rings and serve with Sherry Dressing.

Sherry Dressing

1 3-ounce package cream cheese, softened
2 tablespoons honey
1 tablespoon lemon juice

2 tablespoons sherry
pinch of salt
grated rind of ½ lemon

Work the cream cheese with a fork and gradually stir in honey, lemon juice, sherry, and salt. Add lemon rind and continue mixing until smooth and thoroughly blended.

Yield: 4 servings.

Sherry Berry Salad

This is my beach house salad! The children pick the fruit in the morning, I prepare it in the evening or next day, and part of our dinner is ready when we return from swimming.

¾ cup water
½ cup currant jelly
¾ cup sherry
1 3-ounce package
  blackberry-flavored
  gelatin

¼ cup lemon juice
1 cup fresh
  blackberries
½ cup chopped
  walnuts

Combine water, jelly, and sherry in a small saucepan. Heat the mixture, stirring, until jelly is melted. Bring just to a boil and remove from heat. Add gelatin and lemon juice. Stir to dissolve. Chill until partially set. Stir in blackberries. Chill for 6 hours, or overnight, before serving. Garnish with walnuts.

Yield: 5 to 6 servings.

Blackberry Pancakes

If you freeze the fresh berries individually, you can remove just the amount you want to add to the pancake batter. This is a favorite Sunday evening supper during the winter.

4 egg yolks

2 tablespoons plus ¼ cup sugar

3 tablespoons butter, melted

1½ cups flour, sifted

2 teaspoons baking powder

½ teaspoon salt

1 teaspoon ground cinnamon

1 cup milk

4 egg whites

1 cup blackberries, washed

Combine the egg yolks, 2 tablespoons sugar, and butter in a bowl and beat until well mixed. Sift together the flour, baking powder, salt, and cinnamon and blend into the egg mixture, alternating with milk. Stir the batter until smooth. Beat the egg whites until lightly stiff and fold into batter. Combine blackberries with ¼ cup sugar and stir gently to mix. Fold berries into batter. Drop ¼ cup of batter for each pancake onto a hot, greased griddle and cook the pancakes, turning them once, until they are golden on both sides.

Yield: 14 to 16 pancakes.

Mandarin Cornish Hens

An Orient-inspired blending of fruits and meat that pairs well with any rice dish. For variation, try substituting Spiced Fresh Currants (page 129) for the Spiced Blackberry Relish.

¼ cup soy sauce	½ teaspoon salt
1 garlic clove, crushed	¾ cup Spiced Blackberry Relish (page 42)
½ cup orange juice	
2 tablespoons cooking oil	4 rock cornish hens, 1–1½ pounds each
1 tablespoon tarragon	2 cups mandarin orange slices

Combine soy sauce, crushed garlic, orange juice, oil, tarragon, salt, and Spiced Blackberry Relish. Blend thoroughly and pour into a shallow baking dish. Place hens in the mixture, turning to coat. Cover and marinate for 6 hours in refrigerator, turning frequently. Preheat oven to 425°F. and remove hens to roasting pan. Baste with sauce. Reduce oven temperature to 350°F. and bake hens for 40 minutes, basting often. Add orange slices and continue basting and baking for 20 minutes. Just before serving, place hens under broiler for 2 to 3 minutes. Transfer hens to warm serving platter and surround with rice. Spoon sauce and orange slices over hens.

Yield: 4 servings.

Jenny's Blackberry-Almond Bread

When our youngest child comes home with a small harvest of berries and wants to "make something good," this is it! She takes great pride in serving "her" bread at the evening meal.

1½ cups flour

2 teaspoons baking powder

1 teaspoon salt

¾ cup sugar

1 cup rolled oats

2 tablespoons grated orange rind

¾—1 cup fresh blackberries, washed

½ cup toasted almonds

⅓ cup salad oil

½ cup orange juice

½ cup milk

1 egg

Preheat oven to 350°F.

Sift together flour, baking powder, and salt in a large bowl. Add sugar, oats, orange rind, blackberries, and almonds. Stir to mix. Combine salad oil, orange juice, milk, and egg and add to dry ingredients all at once. Mix only until dry ingredients are moistened. Pour batter into greased and floured 9-by-5-inch loaf pan. Bake in a preheated 350°F. oven for 50 to 60 minutes, or until golden and cake tester inserted in center comes out clean. Cool on wire rack for 10 to 15 minutes before removing from pan. Cool completely before slicing.

Yield: 1 loaf.

Blackberry Jam Spice Cake

 This very moist cake fills the house with the spicy aromas while it bakes.

1 cup butter, softened
2 cups sugar
3 eggs
1½ cups blackberry jam
3 cups flour, sifted
1 teaspoon baking soda
½ teaspoon ground cloves

½ teaspoon ground nutmeg
½ teaspoon allspice
½ teaspoon ground cinnamon
½ teaspoon ginger
1 cup buttermilk
1 cup raisins
1 cup pecans, chopped

Preheat oven to 350°F.

In a large bowl cream together butter and sugar until mixture is fluffy. Beat in eggs and jam. Sift together flour, baking soda, and spices and blend into butter mixture alternately with buttermilk. Stir in raisins and pecans and mix well. Pour into a greased and floured 10-inch tube pan and bake at 350°F. for 45 to 55 minutes, or until cake begins to pull from sides of pan. Remove from pan immediately and cool on wire rack before topping with glaze.

Vanilla Glaze

¼ cup butter, softened
1 cup confectioners' sugar

½ cup milk
1 teaspoon vanilla

In a small bowl cream together butter and confectioners' sugar. Stir in milk and vanilla until mixture is smooth. Dribble over Blackberry Jam Spice Cake.

Yield: 8 to 10 servings.

Blackberry Roly Poly

This old-fashioned dessert was a childhood favorite that I remember from summer vacations in Canada. Emma—a neighboring farm wife—always served it warm from her wood stove with thick cream from the cows I helped milk. The crusty roll is equally delicious if made with raspberries.

4 cups blackberries, washed
½ cup plus 1 teaspoon sugar
juice of ½ lemon
1¾ cups flour
1 teaspoon salt
1 teaspoon baking powder
¼ cup shortening
⅔ cup plus 1 tablespoon milk
2 tablespoons butter, melted
½ teaspoon ground cinnamon
ice cream

Preheat oven to 425°F.

Combine and mix gently the blackberries, ½ cup sugar, and lemon juice. Set aside. In another bowl combine flour, salt, baking powder, and 1 teaspoon sugar. Cut in shortening. Add milk and mix well until dough is soft. Roll dough to a thickness of ⅜ inch on a floured board. Brush with melted butter and sprinkle with cinnamon. Spread blackberry mixture down center of dough, roll up and shape in a ring on a well-greased 14-by-10-inch pan.

Bake in a preheated 425°F. oven for 25 to 35 minutes, or until brown. Garnish with drippings from pan and serve warm with cream.

Yield: 6 to 8 servings.

Blackberry Cobbler

Fruit cobbler—a cake baked with fresh fruit—is traditionally served warm with ice cream. Creamy lemon sauce, however, is a refreshing change and complements the sweetness of the berries.

1 cup sugar
½ cup water
2 cups blackberries, washed
2 tablespoons butter
1 egg

1 cup flour, sifted
1 teaspoon baking powder
⅛ teaspoon salt
⅔ cup milk

Preheat oven to 375°F.

Combine water and ½ cup sugar in a medium saucepan and boil the syrup for 5 minutes. Add blackberries, boil 2 minutes, stirring, and remove from heat. In a bowl cream butter with ½ cup sugar and egg until mixture is well blended. Sift together the flour, baking powder, and salt and add to butter mixture, alternately with milk. Blend until the batter is smooth. Pour the batter into a buttered 1½-quart baking dish. Cover the batter with blackberries and syrup and bake at 375°F. for 45 minutes, or until the crust is golden.

Yield: 6 servings.

Ann's Creamy Blackberry Pie

One of the best cooks I know makes this every summer during blackberry season. It is worth fighting the brambles for this berry and cream combination in a crust!

pastry for 1 crust, 9-inch pie

3 cups blackberries, washed

½ cup sugar

⅛ teaspoon salt

½ teaspoon cinnamon

3 tablespoons flour

1 cup light cream

Preheat the oven to 400°F.

Line a 9-inch pie plate with pastry. Arrange the berries in the unbaked pie shell. Thoroughly combine the sugar, salt, cinnamon, flour, and light cream. Pour the cream mixture over the berries and bake in a preheated 400°F. oven for 35 to 45 minutes, or until the crust is brown and the filling set. Allow the pie to cool slightly on a wire rack before cutting. Serve warm.

Yield: 6 to 8 servings.

Summer Berry Pudding

 This is an old recipe that many people remember watching Grandmother prepare. It tastes as good now as it did then!

slices of stale white bread, crusts removed	1 cup sugar
4 cups blackberries, washed	¼ cup water
	whipped cream

Thoroughly butter a 1-to-1½-quart glass bowl. Line the bowl with the slices of trimmed bread. Trim 1 slice to fit the bottom of the bowl and put in place. Combine the blackberries, sugar, and water in a heavy saucepan and simmer over low heat for 5 minutes, or until the sugar is dissolved and the juices are flowing. Allow the mixture to cool. Spoon enough of the cooled berries into the bread-lined bowl to half fill it and cover completely with a layer of bread slices, buttered on the underside and trimmed to fit together tightly. Pour the remaining juices over the bread. Place a saucer, slightly smaller than the circumference of the bowl, on the pudding and weight it well. Chill the pudding for 24 hours. Unmold onto a chilled serving dish and serve with whipped cream.

Yield: 6 to 8 servings.

Blackberry Bavarian Cream

Because of its delicate lavender color, I like to prepare this dessert in a white soufflé dish. For an extra touch, garnish it with candied violets and sprigs of fresh mint.

4 cups blackberries,
  washed
1½ cups sugar
¼ cup water
1 teaspoon gelatin

½ cup cold milk
4 tablespoons kirsch
2 cups heavy cream,
  lightly whipped
16 lady fingers

In a medium saucepan combine the blackberries, sugar, and water and bring mixture to a boil. Reduce heat and simmer 10 minutes, or until berries are soft. Work the mixture through a fine sieve. In a saucepan sprinkle gelatin over the milk to soften. Place the saucepan in a pan of hot water and stir the gelatin until it is dissolved. Combine the gelatin with the blackberry purée and stir in the kirsch. Refrigerate the mixture until it is slightly thickened. Fold in the whipped cream. Sprinkle the lady fingers with kirsch and arrange them in a 1½-quart soufflé dish. Spoon the blackberry cream in the dish and refrigerate for 3 hours.

Yield: 8 servings.

Blackberry Leather

Fruit leathers are thin sheets of dried puréed fruits. This is pure blackberry flavor and is a good substitute for the usual sweet snacks that children ask for.

4 cups blackberries,
  washed
  honey to taste

Purée the berries and work through a fine sieve to remove seeds. Thoroughly blend desired amount of honey into berry purée. Spray cookie sheets with cookware coating. Pour puréed fruit on sheets and spread to thickness between ⅛ to ¼ inch. Place sheets in warm oven, leaving oven door slightly ajar during drying. Dry for 24 hours, or until leather is moisture-free and firm. Leather may also be processed in a commercial dehydrator. When ready, cut leather into strips, roll up, and wrap in plastic. Store in freezer and thaw for 10 minutes before eating.

Yield: 20 to 25 rolls.

Blackberry Syrup

Delicious over pancakes or puddings, it is also good as a base for milk shakes and sodas.

6 quarts blackberries,
  washed and crushed
3 quarts water
5 cups sugar

Combine the crushed berries and water in a large Dutch oven and bring to a rapid boil. Boil, stirring frequently, for 12 to 15 minutes. Reduce heat and simmer gently for 5 minutes. Strain the mixture through a jelly bag and return the liquid to a large saucepan. Add the sugar. Boil the mixture rapidly for 10 to 15 minutes, or until the syrup begins to thicken slightly. Do not overcook or the syrup will begin to jell. Pour the syrup into hot, sterilized jars and seal with self-sealing lids.

Yield: 3 pints.

Blackberry-Rhubarb Jam

The natural tartness of the rhubarb makes a good marriage with the sweet blackberries.

2 cups blackberries,
washed

4 cups rhubarb,
washed and cut into
1-inch pieces

4 cups sugar

pinch of salt

Combine blackberries, rhubarb, and 2 cups sugar in a large saucepan and bring to a boil. Boil hard for 3 minutes. Add remaining sugar and salt and boil for 15 to 20 minutes, or until the mixture is thick. Ladle into hot, sterilized jars, seal with melted paraffin, and adjust lids.

Yield: 5 half-pints.

Blackberry-Lemon Jam

A favorite addition to Christmas gift baskets.

2 lemons, coarsely
chopped

1½ cups water

6 cups blackberries,
washed

7 cups sugar

Combine lemons and water in a large saucepan and simmer for 20 minutes over moderate heat. Add berries and sugar and cook, stirring frequently, for 20 minutes or until mixture has thickened. Ladle the hot jam into hot, sterilized jars, seal with paraffin, and adjust lids.

Yield: 4 pints.

Spiced Blackberry Relish

 This relish is unusual enough to be an appreciated hostess gift. In addition to serving it with pork or poultry, try some on cream cheese and crackers.

5 quarts blackberries, washed	1 tablespoon ground cinnamon
7 cups light brown sugar	1 teaspoon ground cloves
1 cup malt vinegar	1 teaspoon allspice

Place all the ingredients in a large Dutch oven and bring the mixture to a boil over moderate heat while stirring frequently. Simmer the mixture over low heat for 10 minutes, or until the berries are soft. Ladle the hot mixture into hot, sterilized jars, leaving a ½-inch head space. Adjust lids and store in a dark, cool place.

Yield: 8 to 10 pints.

Blackberry Wine

The deep red color and the full, rich flavor make this one of the most popular fruit wines to prepare and serve. Because it is sweet, you may prefer to serve it with dessert.

4 quarts blackberries, washed and crushed	2 pounds sugar
	1 gallon water
1 cup raisins, chopped	1 packet dry wine yeast

Place the crushed berries, chopped raisins, and sugar in a 2-gallon crock and cover immediately with boiling water. Cover the crock and allow to stand 12 hours, or overnight, at room temperature in a dark area. The next day add the yeast and allow the mixture to ferment 6 days, pushing down the foam and floating berries twice daily. At the end of this period strain through jelly bag and place juice in a clean 1-gallon bottle. Secure fermentation lock on mouth of bottle and allow to stand at room temperature for 2 to 3 weeks, or until fermentation stops. Siphon the wine into a clean 1-gallon storage jar, adding a dry red wine, if necessary, to completely fill jar. Store for 3 months at 50°—55°F. Repeat this process (known as racking) twice more, at 3-month intervals. After the third racking, the wine is ready to be bottled.

Yield: 1 gallon.

Blackberry Brandy

Blackberry Brandy has been used for "medicinal purposes" throughout the years, but you don't have to be sickly to enjoy its warming flavor! A beribboned bottle of brandy is a thoughtful gift that is all the more special because you made it.

4 cups blackberries, washed	1 2-inch stick cinnamon
¾ cup sugar	10 cloves
¾ teaspoon allspice	2 cups brandy

In a clean gallon jar combine blackberries, sugar, and spices. Stir in brandy and adjust cover tightly. Invert jar daily for 4 days or until sugar is completely dissolved. Store in a cool, dry, dark place for at least 2 months. Before serving, strain through cheesecloth. Serve in cordial glasses.

Yield: 3½ cups.

Blender Breakfast

 This frothy, thick drink becomes even more nutritious with the addition of an egg.

1½ cups blackberry
  juice
2 peach halves, peeled
  and thinly sliced

¼ cup honey
1 cup yogurt

Combine blackberry juice, peach slices, and honey in a blender. Blend at high speed until smooth. Add yogurt and blend well.

Yield: 2 servings.

Summer Spritz

 Because blackberries are so abundant in the South, this is a refreshing favorite below the Mason-Dixon line.

1½ cups blackberry
  juice
1 cup orange juice,
  chilled

1 cup pineapple juice,
  chilled
1 cup ginger ale,
  chilled
  orange slices

Thoroughly combine the juices. Add ginger ale. Pour over crushed ice in tall glasses. Garnish with orange slices.

Yield: 2 to 3 servings.

Chapter Four
The All-American Berry

Blueberries and the classic fruit-filled muffins — warm and fragrant from the oven — have always called forth memories of my childhood summertime visits to the Gaspé Peninsula in Canada. While berries of every type grew near the old family home, blueberries seemed to be the most abundant with short, stubby bushes fighting for space on the stony hillsides. Berrying days were among the special events of the summer. We would leave the house midmorning, swinging tin pails heavy with picnic lunches, and walk up the dirt lane to the berry fields. Bending over the low bushes, we would soon have the lunches eaten and the pails mounded high with small, silver-frosted berries. We were careful to leave the green, unripe fruit in place, knowing that the bushes held the promise of other sunny days of berrying and picnicking.

To this day I cannot decide which was more pleasurable—the joyful, warm outings or the wonderful treats made from the fruit. The breads, dumplings, salads, and pies were a featured part of our meals for days after the trip up the lane. When our supply of berries was gone, we knew that the fruit left on the bushes was ready for harvesting and our plans for the next day would be made.

Those small, bluish black balls of flavor, which I picked for so many summers, have been known in North America for centuries. Native to this continent, they were used by Indians in stews and in the curing of wild meat. Blueberries are the featured delicacy for black bears and grizzlies during the summer months and are responsible for the annual wildlife migration up the mountainsides. The animals appear in valley areas where the fruit ripens first and then travel to progressively higher elevations as the berries become plump and juicy.

Although it averages little more than half an inch across, the wild blueberry is considered by bakers and gourmets to be tastier and more desirable than its cultivated sister. The wild plants are found growing throughout North America, with Maine accepting the honor of being the wild blueberry capital of the world.

High-bush and low-bush blueberry are the two varieties found in the wild. The high-bush plant is a shrub with oval leaves and can grow to fifteen feet in height. It thrives in moist, acid, peaty soil and provides easy picking for campers in Cape Cod and other recreational areas. With no thorns to hamper the harvester, pails can be filled easily and rapidly.

Harvesting the low-bush variety is more difficult, especially for someone with back trouble. The plants, about one foot high, with finely serrated leaves, require a lot of bending and stooping. If a person is to suffer a backache, however, the tasty pleasure of hot blueberry muffins might be judged a fair compensation. The low-bush blueberry is generally a hardier plant than the high-bush variety and is found in Canada and the northern regions of the United States.

Commercial cultivation of blueberries was begun in New Jersey at the beginning of the twentieth century, and the United States continues to be the largest producer of the cultivated fruit. For a successful harvest, it is necessary to plant two or more varieties in soil that is acid and rich in humus. Although the plants need a period of cold during the winter, some varieties have been adapted to the South. In the Carolinas there are numerous blueberry farms where, for a fee, families can pick as many berries as they can use. The bushes should be planted in the spring and the harvesting season extends from June to September.

Blueberries and huckleberries, although related and similar in appearance, are geographically divided by the Appalachian Mountains. People who live east of the range refer to all such berries as blueberries, while those living in and west of the mountains call them huckleberries. This may be why Mark Twain named his famous character "Huckleberry" Finn rather than "Blueberry" Finn!

The huckleberry, easily differentiated from the blueberry by the ten large seeds it contains, is generally smaller and more tart than a blueberry. It has many loyal fans, however, who prefer it for baking and preserving.

The huckleberry plant is thought to be one of the oldest living things on earth. An example of its longevity can be found in western Pennsylvania where a single plant, estimated by botanists to be 13,000 years old, covers several square miles. Despite its survival, there has been little effort to cultivate it commercially. Growing abundantly in the wild, the bush is usually one to three feet in height with yellowish green branches and oval leaves. By following the instructions for a particular section of the country, it is possible to grow the plants from seeds.

Another member of the blueberry family is the bilberry, also known in some areas as the whortleberry. This fruit, native to Britain and parts of Europe, is found growing wild in scattered sections of North America. Acid in taste, the berries are used for tarts and jam, while in central Europe they are valued for wine making. The low, ground-hugging plant, found in acid soil near open woodlands, resembles the low-bush blueberry.

Whether your preference is blueberries or huckleberries, the benefits of finding and harvesting the fruit will be the same. You will have a pleasant outing while picking the berries and then enjoy many flavorful recipes using the bounty.

Fresh Fruit Cocktail

Serve this simple but refreshing appetizer in pretty crystal glasses so the summer colors can sparkle through. To complement the appetizer, fill a large crystal bowl with whole fruit to be used as a centerpiece.

1 cup grapefruit
   sections
1 cup orange sections
1 cup fresh pineapple
   chunks
½ cup white grapes

½ cup fresh
   strawberries,
   washed and hulled
1 cup fresh
   blueberries, washed

Prepare the fruit and combine thoroughly. Store in bowl in refrigerator for 1 to 2 hours before serving. Blend in Fruit Sauce just before serving and spoon into long-stemmed glasses.

Fruit Sauce

1 ripe banana, mashed
3 tablespoons honey
¼ teaspoon salt
¼ cup fresh orange
   juice
½ cup buttermilk

Combine all the ingredients and whip with an electric beater until smooth. Chill for 1 to 2 hours before mixing with fresh fruit.

Yield: 6 to 8 servings.

Blueberry-Peach Soup

This soup is good either chilled or warm, although most people seem to prefer it warm. We like it as a "starter" for a summer vegetarian supper when everything seems to ripen in the garden at once.

1 cup white wine
2 cups water
1½ cups grape juice
2 tablespoons lemon juice
⅓ cup quick-cooking tapioca
1 pound peaches, peeled and thinly sliced

2 2-inch sticks cinnamon
a few nutmeg gratings
1 quart blueberries, stemmed and washed
honey to taste
yogurt

In a large Dutch oven combine wine, water, grape juice, lemon juice, and tapioca. Heat to boiling, stirring constantly. Add peaches, cinnamon sticks, and nutmeg. Simmer over low heat until peaches are soft, about 30 minutes. Add blueberries and simmer 10 minutes longer. Remove from heat. Add honey to taste. Serve warm with garnish of yogurt and nutmeg.

Yield: 6 servings.

Creamy Blueberry Soup

This refreshing summer soup can be made the day ahead and refrigerated until serving time. Thin slices of lemon bread are the perfect accompaniment.

1½ tablespoons quick-cooking tapioca

1 cup boiling water

1¼ cups pineapple juice

1¼ cups orange juice

¼ cup sugar

finely grated rind of ½ lemon

¼ teaspoon cinnamon

2 cups fresh blueberries, washed and picked over

¼ cup orange-flavored liqueur

⅓ cup sour cream

fresh mint

Stir the tapioca into boiling water and cook in a medium saucepan, stirring, until the mixture is clear. Stir in the juices, sugar, grated lemon rind, cinnamon, and blueberries. Simmer the mixture over low heat, stirring frequently, for 10 minutes. Remove saucepan from heat and allow the mixture to cool. Stir in the orange-flavored liqueur and sour cream. Blend the mixture in a blender until smooth. Cover and refrigerate for 3 hours. Garnish each serving with a sprig of fresh mint.

Yield: 6 servings.

Chilled Blueberry Soup

 A very successful blending of different fruit flavors. You can experiment with the taste by substituting other brandies, such as apricot or almond.

1½ tablespoons quick-cooking tapioca
¾ cup boiling water
¾ cup pineapple juice
1½ cups grape juice
¼ cup sugar
2½ tablespoons grated orange rind

¼ teaspoon grated nutmeg
¾ cup crushed pineapple
2 cups fresh blueberries, washed
¼ cup cherry brandy
½ cup yogurt

Stir the tapioca into the rapidly boiling water. Cook over moderate heat, stirring, until the mixture is clear. Add pineapple juice, grape juice, sugar, orange rind, nutmeg, crushed pineapple, and blueberries. Cook the mixture over low heat, stirring, for 10 minutes. Remove from heat and allow the mixture to cool. Add brandy and yogurt and blend soup in the blender until smooth. Cover and refrigerate for several hours before serving.

Yield: 6 servings.

Honey Fruit Salad

Fruit salads are a favorite at our house, especially with this Honey Cream Dressing. The recipe came from my Canadian grandmother and made the trips to the berry patches worthwhile.

salad greens
2 avocados, peeled and cut in lengthwise strips
1 tablespoon lemon juice

2 cups cantaloupe balls
1 cup fresh blueberries, washed and picked over
Honey Cream Dressing

Arrange the greens on four individual salad plates. Sprinkle the avocado strips with lemon juice and arrange on the greens. Combine the melon balls and blueberries and mound the mixture on the avocado strips. Serve with Honey Cream Dressing.

Honey Cream Dressing

½ cup honey
4 egg yolks, beaten
  juice of 1 lemon
⅓ cup olive oil

⅓ teaspoon salt
¼ teaspoon paprika
1 cup heavy cream, stiffly whipped

Heat the honey in a small saucepan over moderate heat until very hot. Add the thoroughly beaten egg yolks. Cook for 1 minute, beating continuously. Fold in the lemon juice, oil, salt, paprika, and whipped cream. Refrigerate for 2 hours before serving on Honey Fruit Salad.

Yield: 4 servings.

Patchwork Salad

As pretty as an antique quilt, this salad should be served absolutely fresh with date-nut bread. And for dessert—chocolate cheesecake.

2 large pineapples	1 fresh peach, skinned and sliced
1 orange, peeled and sectioned	1 cup melon balls
1 grapefruit, peeled and sectioned	1 cup sweet cherries, pitted
1 banana, peeled and sliced	1½ cups fresh blueberries, washed and picked over

Halve pineapples lengthwise through the green tops. Scoop out fruit and cut into cubes. Prepare fruit listed above to total approximately two quarts. Mix fruit well and spoon into pineapple shells. Serve with Sour Cream Dressing.

Sour Cream Dressing

2 tablespoons fresh orange juice	1 tablespoon lime juice
1 teaspoon soy sauce	½ cup mayonnaise
½ teaspoon sugar	½ cup sour cream
¼ teaspoon Tabasco sauce	

With electric beater blend orange juice, soy sauce, sugar, Tabasco, and lime juice into mayonnaise. Stir in sour cream and blend well. Chill before serving with Patchwork Salad.

Yield: 4 servings.

Molded Blueberry Salad

An interesting salad that always wins compliments, this creamy blending of several fruit flavors can be prepared hours before your guests' arrival. Because of the color and texture of this salad, it should properly be called Blueberry Cloud!

1 cup hot water
2 cups pineapple juice
1 package (6 ounce) lemon gelatin
1 large banana, mashed

2 tablespoons sugar
1 pint fresh blueberries, washed
1 cup heavy cream, whipped

In a bowl combine hot water with pineapple juice. Add gelatin and stir until dissolved. Chill in refrigerator until partially thickened. Fold in mashed banana, sugar, blueberries, and whipped cream. Turn into 2-quart mold and refrigerate until set.

Yield: 8 to 10 servings.

Fruited Chicken Salad

Serve a make-ahead luncheon of Fruited Chicken Salad with spiced peaches, and an easy dessert of strawberries mixed with softened pineapple sherbet. This is an easy, impressive meal without fuss.

salad greens
3 cups cooked chicken, diced
¾ cup celery, diced
1 cup fresh orange sections

½ cup almonds, slivered
1 cup fresh blueberries, washed
½ cup seedless grapes, halved

Line a salad bowl with greens. Combine the remaining ingredients and place on top of the greens. Chill. Just before serving, toss with Celery Seed Dressing.

Yield: 6 to 8 servings.

Celery Seed Dressing

1 teaspoon dry mustard
1 teaspoon salt
½ teaspoon paprika
1 tablespoon celery seed
2 drops Tabasco sauce

½ teaspoon grated onion
2 tablespoons honey
⅓ cup white vinegar
1 cup salad oil

Combine all the ingredients in a bowl and beat thoroughly. Chill for several hours. Toss with Fruited Chicken Salad.

Yield: 1½ cups.

Blueberry Palachinki

This is traditionally served as a dessert but I like it as a luncheon entrée. The crepes can be made ahead, frozen, and reheated in the oven just before serving.

3 eggs
1 cup milk
1¼ cups all-purpose flour
1 teaspoon sugar
¼ teaspoon salt
1 teaspoon vanilla extract

1 cup club soda, freshly opened
4—6 tablespoons butter
1½ cup blueberry jam
1 cup sour cream
powdered sugar

Preheat oven to 200°F.

Beat the eggs lightly with the milk in a large bowl. Stir in the flour, sugar, salt, and vanilla extract. Continue to stir until the batter is smooth. Set aside for 1 hour. Just before making pancakes, stir in the club soda. Melt 1 teaspoon of butter in an 8-inch crepe skillet. When the foam subsides, ladle in enough batter to cover the bottom of the skillet thinly and tilt the skillet from side to side to spread it evenly. Cook for 2 to 3 minutes, or until lightly browned on the bottom. Turn pancake to brown other side. When the pancake is done, spread 2 table-spoons jam across the center of the face and roll it loosely into a cylinder. Place the palachinki in a buttered baking dish in a preheated 200°F. oven to keep warm. Add butter to skillet as needed and continue making the pancakes. When ready to serve, arrange palachinki on plates, garnish each with a tablespoon of sour cream and sprinkle with powdered sugar.

Yield: 12 to 14 palachinki.

Classic Blueberry
Griddle Cakes

Some people like to serve this American favorite with Huckleberry Syrup, but that always seems like too much of a good thing!

1 cup flour, sifted	1 cup milk
2 tablespoons sugar	3 tablespoons butter or margarine, melted
1½ teaspoons baking powder	
½ teaspoon salt	1½ cups fresh blueberries, washed and picked over
1 egg, well beaten	

Into a medium bowl sift together the flour, sugar, baking powder, and salt. Combine the beaten egg, milk, and melted butter and add to the dry ingredients. Beat the mixture only until the ingredients are combined. The batter will be lumpy. Add the berries. Drop the batter by ¼ cupfuls onto a hot, greased griddle or heavy skillet. Cook until bubbles form on surface and edges become dry. Turn and cook 2 minutes longer, or until browned on underside. Serve with maple syrup.

Yield: 10 griddle cakes.

Blueberry Omelet

Even people who do not like eggs like this omelet. It is perfect for a Sunday evening supper with a dessert of Pink Peach Compote.

4 eggs, at room
temperature,
separated

½ teaspoon
granulated sugar

dash of salt

2½ tablespoons heavy
cream

1 tablespoon butter

4 ounces cream
cheese, softened

Blueberry Omelet
Sauce

powdered sugar

In a small bowl beat the egg whites until stiff. In another bowl beat the egg yolks, sugar, salt, and 1 tablespoon heavy cream with a fork. Gently fold whites into yolk mixture. Melt the butter over low heat in an omelet pan. Add the omelet mixture. Reduce heat as the omelet begins to color on the bottom. Shake to loosen but continue cooking until the center is spongy. Place omelet on heated platter. Mix softened cream cheese with 1½ tablespoons heavy cream and spoon onto center of omelet. Cover with half the omelet sauce. Gently fold omelet in half and spoon on the rest of the sauce. Dust with powdered sugar.

Blueberry Omelet Sauce

1 cup fresh
blueberries, washed
and picked over

3 tablespoons sugar

1 tablespoon
cornstarch

dash of salt

¼ cup water

1 tablespoon orange
juice

1 teaspoon grated
orange rind

Combine all the ingredients in a medium saucepan. Boil
gently over moderate heat for 5 minutes. Serve warm
with Blueberry Omelet.

Yield: 2 servings.

Huckleberry Breakfast Cake

When our children were very young, we vacationed in a camper that had all the amenities—including a small oven. This is how we used our harvest of the previous day. Because it keeps well, it is a good addition to a picnic basket.

¼ cup butter, softened
¾ cup sugar
1 egg
½ cup milk
2 cups flour
2 teaspoons baking powder

½ teaspoon salt
2 cups huckleberries, stemmed and washed
1 cup walnuts, chopped

Preheat oven to 375°F.

Cream together butter and sugar. Add egg and milk and beat until smooth. Sift together flour, baking powder, and salt. Add huckleberries and nuts to dry ingredients and toss gently. Combine thoroughly with butter mixture. Pour batter into greased and floured 9-inch square pan. Sprinkle with Crumb Topping and bake in preheated 375°F. oven for 40 to 45 minutes, or until cake tester inserted in the center comes out clean.

Crumb Topping

½ cup brown sugar, packed
1 teaspoon cinnamon

2 tablespoons flour
2 tablespoons butter, softened

Mix together sugar, cinnamon, and flour. Cut in butter to form coarse crumbs. Sprinkle on top of Huckleberry Breakfast Cake and bake in oven.

Yield: 6 to 8 servings.

Blueberry-Orange Bread

 For holiday giving, divide the batter into smaller pans to make tea loaves. They can be made in early December—before the hectic rush—and stored in the freezer until needed. To prevent the berries from sinking to the bottom of the bread, remember to toss them in a little flour before adding to the batter.

2 tablespoons butter, melted
¼ cup milk
½ cup fresh orange juice
3½ teaspoons grated orange rind
½ teaspoon vanilla
1 egg
1 cup sugar
2 cups flour

¼ teaspoon baking soda
1 teaspoon baking powder
½ teaspoon salt
1½ cups blueberries, stemmed and washed
½ cups pecans, chopped

Preheat oven to 350°F.

In a small bowl combine melted butter, milk, orange juice, orange rind, and vanilla. In a large bowl beat egg and sugar until light and fluffy. Sift together flour, baking soda, baking powder, and salt. Add dry ingredients to the egg mixture, alternately with the juice. Beat until smooth. Gently fold in berries and pecans. Pour the batter into a lightly greased 9-by-5-by-3-inch loaf pan. Bake in a preheated 350°F. oven for 1 hour, or until a cake tester inserted in the center comes out clean. Allow the bread to stand in the pan for 5 minutes before turning onto a rack to cool. When thoroughly cooled, wrap in foil and let sit overnight before cutting.

Yield: 1 loaf.

Blueberry Crisp

Particular foods often trigger childhood memories. For some people it may be applesauce, for others it may be molasses cookies. For me—it is this Blueberry Crisp.

4 cups blueberries, washed
1 teaspoon grated lemon rind
1 cup quick rolled oats, uncooked
1 teaspoon ground cinnamon

½ cup flour
¾ cup brown sugar, firmly packed
½ cup butter, softened
vanilla ice cream

Preheat oven to 350°F.

Arrange blueberries in a 10-inch-square baking dish. Sprinkle with lemon rind. In a bowl combine rolled oats, cinnamon, flour, and brown sugar. Cut in butter until evenly mixed and crumbly. Sprinkle over the berries. Bake in a preheated 350°F. oven for 25 to 30 minutes. Serve warm with vanilla ice cream.

Yield: 6 servings.

Blueberry Gingerbread

 This gingerbread is my therapy on a rainy day. First, there is the fun of making it and then the pleasure of eating it. Try it with lemon sauce.

1 cup molasses
1 cup sour cream
½ cup brown sugar, firmly packed
2 eggs
2¼ cups flour
2 teaspoons baking soda
½ teaspoon salt

1 teaspoon ground ginger
¼ teaspoon ground nutmeg
¼ teaspoon ground cloves
1¼ cups blueberries, floured

Preheat oven to 350°F.

Stir together molasses and sour cream. Stir in brown sugar and beat until light. Add eggs and beat well. Sift together flour, baking soda, salt, ginger, nutmeg, and ground cloves. Add dry ingredients to the molasses mixture and beat until smooth. Fold in floured blueberries. Pour batter into greased 13-by-9-by-3-inch pan and bake in preheated 350°F. oven for 35 minutes, or until a cake tester inserted in the center comes out clean.

Yield: 10 to 12 servings.

Blueberry Nut Ice Cream

 The color of this ice cream is as soft as a summer day. For an elegant dessert, serve it on cantaloupe wedges.

1½ cups sugar	1 teaspoon vanilla
4 eggs, beaten	½ teaspoon salt
5 cups blueberries, pureed	grated rind of 1 lemon
3 cups heavy cream	1½ cups walnuts, chopped
1 cup light cream	

Add sugar to beaten eggs in a large bowl. Stir in puréed blueberries, heavy and light creams, vanilla, and salt. Mix thoroughly. Add grated lemon rind and chopped nuts. Pour the mixture into freezer can of ice-cream maker. Pack freezer with chopped ice and rock salt.

Yield: 3 quarts.

Peaches and Cream

A cliché that gets even better with the addition of blueberries! This is an elegant and easy dessert.

1 cup blueberries, washed and picked over

2 tablespoons almond-flavored liqueur

2 tablespoons honey

1 cup heavy cream

6 peaches, skinned, stoned, and sliced

¼ cup almonds, slivered

In a blender purée the blueberries with the liqueur and honey. In a bowl whip the cream until it holds stiff peaks and fold in the blueberry purée. Arrange the prepared peach slices on dessert plates and spoon the blueberry cream over them. Garnish each serving with a sprinkle of almonds.

Yield: 6 servings.

Jane's Blueberry Cheese Pie

This pie is an adaptation of one I tasted during my first visit to North Carolina. The thing that makes it special and southern is the pecans.

8 ounces (1 large package) cream cheese, softened

1 tablespoon heavy cream

1 teaspoon grated lemon rind

1 cup powdered sugar

⅛ teaspoon salt

3 eggs

1 cup blueberries, washed and picked over

1 graham cracker pie crust

1 cup pecans, chopped

Preheat oven to 350°F.

Allow cheese to soften at room temperature. In a bowl combine the cheese, heavy cream, and lemon rind until smooth. Add sugar, salt, and eggs and blend. Beat for 5 minutes, or until mixture is smooth and creamy. Gently fold in the blueberries. Cover the graham cracker pie crust with the chopped pecans. Pour the cheese mixture over the chopped nuts. Bake in a preheated 350°F. oven for 30 minutes, or until set. Remove from oven and allow to stand until cold.

Glaze

¼ cup granulated sugar

1½ tablespoons cornstarch

dash of salt

½ cup water

1 cup blueberries

In a small saucepan mix together sugar, cornstarch, and salt. Add water and blueberries. Bring to a boil, stirring. Cook over moderate heat, stirring, for 5 minutes, or until clear and thickened. Spoon glaze over pie and refrigerate for several hours.

Yield: 6 to 8 servings.

Blueberry Dumplings

Because the preparation is easy and the results delicious, this is a good dessert to include in your camping menu. It is fun to experiment with this recipe by adding some other fruits, particularly fresh diced peaches.

2 cups water
4 cups blueberries
1 cup plus 3
  teaspoons sugar
½ lemon, thinly sliced
1½ cups flour

1½ teaspoons baking
  powder
½ teaspoon salt
2 eggs, beaten
½ cup milk
  cream

In a deep skillet combine the water, blueberries, 1 cup sugar, and the lemon slices. Over moderate heat, bring the mixture to a rolling boil. In a large bowl sift together the flour, 3 teaspoons sugar, baking powder, and salt. Add eggs and milk and stir until smooth. Drop batter by tablespoons into boiling berries. Cover, reduce heat, and simmer the mixture for 10 to 15 minutes. Transfer the dumplings to individual serving dishes and spoon the sauce over each. Serve warm with a pitcher of cream.

Yield: 6 servings.

Blueberry-Apple Conserve

This conserve makes a supper of sliced, cold pork very special.

4 cups blueberries, washed

4 cups apples, peeled and chopped

3 cups granulated sugar

2½ cups brown sugar

½ cup raisins

1 lemon, finely chopped

½ teaspoon cinnamon

½ cup almonds, slivered

Combine all the ingredients, except the almonds, in a large Dutch oven over moderate heat. Bring the mixture to a boil slowly, stirring frequently, until the sugar is dissolved. Cook rapidly, stirring, for 20 minutes, or until mixture is thick. Stir in almonds during the last few minutes of cooking. Ladle the hot conserve into hot, sterilized jars and adjust the lids. Store in a dark, dry place.

Yield: 6 half-pints.

Blueberry Jam

For a special gift, at Christmastime, or any time, arrange a pretty jar of this jam and a tea loaf of Blueberry-Orange Bread (page 63) in an old-fashioned berry basket decorated with holiday ribbons.

1½ quarts ripe
  blueberries,
  stemmed and
  washed
2 tablespoons lemon
  juice

7 cups sugar
1 teaspoon cinnamon
1 bottle liquid fruit
  pectin

Slightly crush the berries, one layer at a time. Into a large Dutch oven measure 4½ cups of the crushed fruit. Stir in lemon juice. Combine sugar and cinnamon with fruit in pot and mix thoroughly. Bring the mixture to a full rolling boil over high heat. Boil hard for 1 minute, stirring constantly. Remove from heat and immediatcly stir in liquid pectin. Skim off foam and stir constantly for 5 minutes. Ladle the hot jam into hot, sterilized jars, leaving a ½-inch head space. Cover with melted paraffin. Store in a dark, dry place.

Yield: 9 half-pints.

Huckleberry Syrup

 Huckleberry syrup running over waffles or pancakes on a cold February morning seems an ideal way to recall summer walks in the country.

2 cups huckleberry juice	1 tablespoon lemon juice
1¼ cups sugar	1½ cups white corn syrup (clear)

Extract juice from whole, cooked, unsweetened berries, as for jelly. Heat juice to boiling in a medium saucepan. Add sugar and stir until dissolved. Stir in lemon juice and corn syrup. Heat to boiling, stirring. Reduce heat and simmer for 5 minutes, or until syrup thickens. Remove from heat and pour into hot, sterilized jars and seal.

Yield: 4 half-pints.

Blueberry-Pineapple Float

I like this for a summer lunch when the day is too warm for anything more substantial. The taste can be varied by substituting other juices and sherbets.

1¼ cups blueberries, washed	2 cups yogurt, chilled
1 cup pineapple juice, chilled	¼ cup milk
	½ cup pineapple sherbet

Combine 1 cup blueberries, pineapple juice, yogurt, and milk in a blender. Blend thoroughly until smooth. Pour into 2 large, chilled glasses. Top each serving with ¼ cup pineapple sherbet. Garnish with remaining berries.

Yield: 2 servings.

Blueberry Ice Cream Shake

 Although I have never met a milk shake I did not like, this one seems to outshine them all! Its frothy, delicate flavor is perfect for a hot July afternoon in the hammock.

1½ cups heavy cream, whipped

1 egg

¾ cup fresh blueberries, washed

2 tablespoons sugar

½ teaspoon vanilla extract

2 cups milk

½ pint vanilla ice cream

grated nutmeg

In a chilled bowl whip heavy cream until stiff. Set aside. Combine egg, blueberries, sugar, vanilla extract, and milk in a blender. Blend thoroughly until smooth. Gently fold berry mixture into whipped cream. Pour into 6 tall glasses and top each with a scoop of ice cream. Garnish each serving with nutmeg.

Yield: 6 servings.

Blueberry Wine

The small, wild berries make a more flavorful wine than the cultivated varieties. The color and body of this wine improves greatly if you age it for a year.

4 quarts blueberries, crushed	1 packet dry wine yeast
6 quarts boiling water	1 cup raisins
2½ pounds sugar	2 vitamin C tablets, crushed

Place the berries in a 3-gallon crock and cover immediately with boiling water. Add sugar and stir until dissolved. Allow mixture to cool to room temperature. Stir in yeast. Add raisins. Cover the crock with plastic wrap. Allow the crock to stand in a dark place, at room temperature for 5 days, pressing down the foam and floating berries twice daily. At the end of this period strain through jelly bag, squeezing well to extract all juice. Pour the liquid into sterilized gallon jugs, leaving a 4-inch head space. Secure fermentation lock on mouth of each bottle. Allow to stand in the dark, undisturbed, at room temperature for 2 to 4 weeks, or until fermentation stops. Siphon the wine into clean 1-gallon storage jars, adding any red wine, if necessary, to completely fill jars to the top. To each gallon, add 1 crushed vitamin C tablet as an antioxidant.* Store for 3 months at 50 to 55°F. Repeat the siphoning process twice more, at 3-month intervals. Bottle the wine after final racking in the ninth month.

Yield: 1½ gallons.

* Because certain wines will pick up oxygen, resulting in an undesirable taste, it is advisable to add vitamin C as an antioxidant.

Chapter Five
The Bouncing Berry of the Bog

Bowls of freshly cooked cranberry sauce stand near the holiday turkey. Garlands of red berries hang in graceful loops on the Christmas tree while cranberry-scented candles glow softly in front of mirrors, filling the house with the sights and smells of festivity.

Although cranberries will probably always be associated with pilgrims and winter holidays, they have recently gained an everyday popularity that is not confined to the traditional sauce. Whether cooked in stews or baked with chicken, the marblelike berries are extremely versatile and turn an ordinary meal into a celebration.

The North American Indians, however, were not thinking of parties and holidays when they used the native red *ibimi*—bitter berry—long before the arrival of the first pilgrims. With survival their main concern, the Indians made a mixture of crushed wild berries and melted fat with which they covered deer meat. Pemmican, as this dried staple of the diet was called, would keep for long periods of time without spoilage and sustained them throughout the severe New England winters.

Because the cranberry possessed the valuable quality of maintaining freshness for long periods, the colonists soon adopted the berry for their own needs and learned how to use it. Cranberries, high in vitamin C, were carried in barrels of cold water on long ship voyages to be used as a scurvy preventative for the crew. In 1677, to appease an angry King Charles II, the Massachusetts colony sent ten barrels of the red berries across the ocean in slow-moving vessels. On that same voyage were also sent three thousand codfish and it does not take much imagination to guess which gift reached the shores of England in better condition!

The red fruit, recognized as an important part of the colonial diet, was gathered each fall by entire families. One Cape Cod settlement, in 1773, levied a fine of one dollar on any person caught picking more than a quart of the berries before September 20. After paying such a high price for his wrongdoing, the offender suffered the additional insult of having his berries taken from him!

The cranberry received its original name of "craneberry" from the pilgrims, who thought the pink blossom resembled the head and neck of the crane. This imagery was further enhanced when delicate, long-necked cranes were annually seen standing in the bogs, eating the treasured fruit.

The creeping vine that produces the firm, waxy-coated berries can be six inches to two feet in length and thrives in the marshy areas of the coast. Small, oval leaves growing on alternate sides of the stem provide an appropriate background for the pink blossoms that appear in profusion in early summer. The green berries ripen to a Christmas red in late September or October and serve as a natural harbinger of the holiday feasts to come.

Each of the several varieties of wild cranberry bushes differs slightly in appearance, but all produce the firm, red berry that is unpleasant tasting when raw. The popular snowball bush, found in gardens and lawns, is a cultivated form of the wild cranberry tree that has been made to produce only sterile flowers. All the wild cranberries are found along the coastal regions of North America and cling to the bushes throughout the winter. Like their cultivated relative, the wild berries lose their bitter flavor when cooked with sugar and can serve as an accompaniment to a meal or an integral part of the main course.

Because cranberries need a swamplike environment, most cultivation is commercially done. Autumn tourists in Wisconsin, Oregon, Washington, New Jersey, and Massachusetts frequently have the pleasure of watching the harvesting of the bright red crops. If frost threatens as harvesttime approaches, the water gates of the bogs are opened and the area is flooded over to prevent damage to the fruit. Local residents benefit from this practice when they use these same areas as ice-skating rinks during the winter.

Perhaps the most distinctive characteristic of the cranberry is the unique method by which its ripeness is judged. When dropped on a hard floor, the berries—at their peak of perfection—will bounce several inches into the air, while the bruised or rotten fruit remains motionless. This discovery led to the invention of the first cranberry separator, the forerunner of the models used in contemporary processing.

When the relatively inexpensive "bouncing berries" become available in early autumn, I buy an extra supply to store in the freezer. This versatile fruit brightens many winter meals and, of course, we need some to decorate the Christmas tree!

Candied Cranberries

Perfect on an appetizer tray with olives and miniature cheese balls because they are so festive and tasty. They can also be used to garnish the holiday roast.

1 cup large
  cranberries, washed
  and picked over
1 cup sugar
1 cup water
  granulated sugar

Wash and dry the cranberries and prick each one with a needle to prevent the skins from popping. In a saucepan combine the sugar and water and boil the syrup until it spins a fine thread, or a candy thermometer registers 234°. Add the berries to the syrup and cook them until the thermometer reads 250°, or a drop of syrup forms a hard ball when dropped in cold water. Remove the berries with a slotted spoon to a sheet of wax paper and allow them to stand until dry. Roll the cranberries in granulated sugar.

Yield: 1 cup.

Cranberry Fritters

 The batter can be prepared early in the day and refrigerated until cooking time for these crispy hors d'oeuvres. Serve them hot for a delicious change from the usual trays of crackers and cheese.

2 cups cranberries, washed and picked over	2 teaspoons grated lemon rind
½ cup water	½ teaspoon salt
½ cup sugar	dash of mace
1 tablespoon butter, melted	1 cup cracker crumbs
	coarse salt

Combine the cranberries and water in a saucepan. Cook over medium heat until the berries are soft. Force the cranberries through a sieve. Add the sugar, butter, lemon rind, salt, and mace to the purée. Stir in the cracker crumbs until a paste is formed. Drop the batter by teaspoonfuls into hot, deep fat (370 °F.) and cook the fritters until they are golden on both sides. Drain them on paper toweling and sprinkle with coarse salt.

Yield: 10 to 14 fritters.

Cranberry Wing Appetizers

If you are lucky, there might be a few of these appetizers left over for lunch the next day—but don't plan on it! Men, especially, seem to gather around this dish.

¾ cup flour
1 tablespoon salt
¼ teaspoon pepper
24 chicken wings, tips removed and broken at joints
½ cup butter
¼ cup sugar
¾ teaspoon curry powder

⅛ teaspoon ground ginger
1 cup whole cranberry sauce
¼ cup vinegar
1 tablespoon molasses
¾ teaspoon Worcestershire sauce
dash of soy sauce

Preheat oven to 375°F.

Combine flour, salt, and pepper in a plastic bag. Add 2 or 3 wings at a time and shake to coat. Melt butter in 14-by-10-by-2-inch baking dish. Place wings in pan, turning once to butter surface. Bake in preheated 375°F. oven for 50 minutes. In a saucepan combine the remaining ingredients. Bring to a boil, reduce heat, and simmer for 3 minutes. Add the sauce to the chicken at the end of 50 minutes, reduce oven temperature to 325°F., and continue to bake for 10 minutes. Remove chicken wings and sauce to blazer pan of chafing dish and serve hot.

Yield: 4 dozen.

Chafing Dish Ham

 In addition to being a delicious appetizer, this makes a good luncheon entrée when served with rice and a green salad. The sauce can also be served warm over slices of baked ham or pork tenderloin.

½ cup sugar
1 cup water
2 cups fresh cranberries
1 cup brown sugar, firmly packed
1 tablespoon cornstarch
1 teaspoon salt
½ teaspoon paprika

¼ teaspoon ground ginger
1 teaspoon curry powder
½ cup vinegar
1 cup pineapple chunks, undrained
1 teaspoon Worcestershire sauce
ham, cooked and cubed

In a saucepan combine the sugar and water. Bring to a boil, stirring, and boil for 5 minutes. Add the fresh cranberries and cook for 5 minutes. Drain off the liquid. Add to the cranberries all the remaining ingredients, except the ham. Cook over moderate heat, stirring constantly, until thickened. Add ham cubes and simmer over low heat until meat is heated through. Transfer mixture to blazer pan of chafing dish.

Yield: 4 cups sauce.

Cranberry-Pumpkin Soup

Two native American foods blend successfully in this thick, creamy soup that is just right for brisk autumn days. To be as frugal as the pilgrims, make use of the entire pumpkin by carving Halloween jack-o'-lanterns, cube the pulp for soup, and roast and salt the seeds for snacking.

3 cups pumpkin, diced, or 2 cups canned pumpkin

2 cups raw cranberries, mashed

2½ cups chicken broth

½ cup onion, finely chopped

2 tablespoons butter

1½ cups scalded milk

¼ teaspoon nutmeg
salt and pepper

¾ cup heavy cream

Combine pumpkin, mashed cranberries, and broth in a large Dutch oven. Bring mixture to a boil and cook over moderate heat until fruit is tender. Remove from heat and cool. Sauté onion in butter until soft. Add onion to pumpkin-cranberry mixture and purée in the blender. Return the purée to heat, and stir in scalded milk and nutmeg. Season with salt and pepper. Blend in cream (do not boil), remove from heat, and serve at once.

Yield: 6 to 8 servings.

Sweet and Sour Soup

 You can add whatever vegetables you happen to have on hand but, because the cooking time is short, the vegetables should be shredded or finely cut.

2 cups cranberry juice
6 beef bouillon cubes
4 cups water
1 teaspoon chopped
  chives
1 cup green cabbage,
  shredded
½ cup carrot,
  shredded

½ cup green beans,
  French cut
1 cup ham, cooked
  and cubed
¼ teaspoon
  Worcestershire
  sauce
pepper

Combine all the ingredients in a large saucepan. Simmer the mixture, covered, over low heat for 30 to 40 minutes, or until the vegetables are tender.

Yield: 4 servings.

Cranberry Wine Salad

This sparkling red molded salad becomes the center of attention on a buffet table when it is garnished with Candied Cranberries (page 78) and bunches of sugar-frosted grapes.

1 3-ounce package strawberry-flavored gelatin
1 cup boiling water
1 cup mixed melon balls

1 grapefruit, sectioned
¼ cup pink Chablis
1 cup fresh cranberries, ground in meat grinder or food processor

Dissolve gelatin in boiling water. Stir in melon balls and grapefruit sections. Stir in Chablis and chill until partially set. Fold in ground cranberries. Turn into 1-quart mold and chill until firm.

Yield: 6 servings.

Christmas Salad

 This salad is a traditional part of our Christmas dinner every year. It is so good that I also make it for "bring a dish" suppers with friends.

1 cup cranberries

1 orange, quartered and seeded

2 3-ounce packages lime-flavored gelatin

3 cups boiling water

1 20-ounce can crushed pineapple

1 cup seedless green grapes, halved

1 cup celery, diced

1 cup walnuts, chopped

1 cup heavy cream, whipped

Work cranberries and orange through food grinder or food processor. Dissolve lime gelatin in boiling water. Stir in undrained crushed pineapple, cranberries, orange, grapes, celery, and walnuts. Refrigerate until partially set. Fold whipped cream into gelatin mixture and pour into 2-quart soufflé dish. Chill until firm.

Yield: 8 to 10 servings.

Cranberry Cream Salad

A different version of the classic Waldorf salad, this crunchy and colorful combination is a favorite of both children and adults—even those who ordinarily disdain salads with marshmallows.

2 cups cranberries
3 cups miniature
  marshmallows
¾ cup sugar
1 cup tart apple, diced
1 cup celery, diced
½ cup seedless green
  grapes

½ cup walnuts,
  chopped
pinch of salt
1 cup heavy cream,
  whipped
lettuce
grapes

Grind cranberries in food grinder or food processor and combine with marshmallows and sugar. Cover and refrigerate overnight. The following day add apple, celery, grapes, walnuts, and salt. Fold in whipped cream and chill for 3 hours. Mound in individual lettuce cups and garnish with grapes.

Yield: 8 servings.

Cranberry Beef Stew

 A good cold-weather dinner that fills the house with a wonderful aroma. Serve it with rice or noodles and a salad.

3 tablespoons butter	4 cups cranberries
½ cup chopped onion	1 tablespoon sugar
2 cloves garlic, chopped	1 teaspoon thyme
	3 sprigs fresh parsley
3 pounds lean beef, cut in 2-inch cubes	1 bay leaf
flour	½ cup mushrooms, sliced
salt and pepper	1 cup celery, diced
2 cups beef bouillon	6 carrots, peeled and cut in half lengthwise
1 cup dry, red wine	
1 cup tomatoes, peeled, seeded, and chopped	

In a large Dutch oven on top of the stove, melt the butter and sauté the chopped onion and garlic until softened. Roll the beef cubes in flour, seasoned with salt and pepper, and brown the beef over high heat for 3 to 5 minutes, adding more butter as necessary. Add remaining ingredients, except celery and carrots, and simmer the mixture, covered, for 1¼ hours. Add the celery and carrots and continue cooking, covered, for 45 minutes, or until meat and vegetables are tender.

Yield: 6 to 8 servings.

Cranberry-Stuffed Pork Crown Roast

This is the most elegant of roasts so the stuffing should be special too. Serve it with oven-browned potatoes, spinach soufflé, and Cranberry Cream Salad.

1 5½–6 pound (12–14 ribs) crown roast of pork

1¼ teaspoons salt
¼ teaspoon pepper
spiced crab apples

Cranberry Stuffing

3½ cups dry bread cubes
2 cups cranberries, chopped
¼ cup sugar
2½ tablespoons finely chopped onion
3 tablespoons grated orange peel

1 teaspoon salt
¼ teaspoon thyme
¼ teaspoon parsley
¼ teaspoon marjoram
½ cup butter, melted
½ cup orange juice

Preheat oven to 325 °F.

Place roast in roasting pan with rib bones up. Season meat with salt and pepper. Wrap tips of bones in foil to prevent excess browning. Insert meat thermometer in thickest part of meat, being sure it does not rest on bone or fat. Do not add water. Roast at 325°F. for 2 hours, uncovered. Prepare Cranberry Stuffing by thoroughly mixing all the ingredients. Fill center of roast with stuffing and roast 1½ to 2 hours longer, or until meat is well done and meat thermometer registers 170°F. When ready to serve, remove foil and cover each bone end with a spiced crab apple.

Yield: 6 to 8 servings.

Veal Chops in Wine

This is a satisfying meat dish for anyone—especially someone who may be diet-conscious. Complete the meal with a rice casserole and fresh fruit salad.

2 tablespoons flour
½ teaspoon salt
¼ teaspoon pepper
4 veal loin chops
1 clove garlic, finely chopped
1 tablespoon butter
1 small onion, finely sliced
½ cup fresh mushrooms, sliced
1 cup fresh cranberries, washed and picked over
1 cup tomatoes, peeled, seeded, and chopped
½ cup white wine

Combine flour, salt, and pepper. Coat the chops with the flour mixture. In a skillet melt the butter. Place the floured meat and chopped garlic in the skillet and brown the chops on both sides over medium heat. Add onion, mushrooms, cranberries, tomatoes, and wine. Cover, reduce heat, and simmer for 1 to 1¼ hours, or until meat is tender.

Yield: 4 servings.

Cranberry Stuffed Pork Chops

An easy supper with a flair! Serve with Currant Sweet Potatoes with Apples for a hearty, cold-weather meal.

6 loin pork chops, cut
   1½ to 2 inches
   thick

2 cups soft bread
   cubes

1 cup fresh
   cranberries, cut in
   half

3 tablespoons
   chopped onion

¼ teaspoon salt

¼ teaspoon poultry
   seasoning

4 tablespoons orange
   juice

   salt and pepper

Preheat oven to 325 °F.

Cut a deep slit or pocket in pork chops, cutting almost to the bone. In a large mixing bowl combine bread cubes, cranberries, onion, salt, poultry seasoning, and orange juice. Mix well. Fill the meat pockets with stuffing. Close the pockets with toothpicks and place chops in baking dish. Mound extra stuffing on each chop. Sprinkle with salt and pepper. Cover and bake in preheated 325 °F. oven for 1¼ to 1½ hours until tender.

Yield: 6 servings.

Honey Cranberry Chicken

Cape Cod not only produces cranberries but delicious recipes for cooking the "bouncing berries." In this recipe you can use either the commercially prepared sauce or your own.

2 tablespoons butter
½ cup honey
¼ cup spicy brown
   mustard
1 teaspoon salt

1 teaspoon curry
   powder
1 3-pound fryer
   chicken, cut up
1½ cups whole
   cranberry sauce

Preheat oven to 375 °F.

Melt butter in a 9-by-12-inch baking dish. Stir in honey, mustard, salt, and curry powder. Place chicken in dish and turn once to coat, leaving skin side up for baking. Bake in preheated 375 °F. oven for 45 minutes. Remove from oven and stir in cranberry sauce. Return to oven and continue baking for 15 minutes.

Yield: 4 servings.

Holiday Sausage Stuffing *

Because I serve roast turkey frequently, I have experimented with many different stuffings. This is one of the best! Store enough cranberries in the freezer so you can prepare this anytime.

1 pound bulk pork sausage	1 egg, beaten
½ cup celery, chopped	¼ cup butter, melted
¼ cup onion, chopped	¼ teaspoon poultry seasoning
8 slices white bread, toasted and cubed	¼ teaspoon sage
¾ cup cranberries, chopped	⅛ teaspoon salt
	freshly ground pepper

In a skillet cook sausage, onion, and celery until meat is lightly browned and vegetables are tender. Drain mixture on several thicknesses of paper toweling. In a large bowl combine meat mixture with remaining ingredients and mix well. This makes enough stuffing for a 12-to-14-pound turkey.

*This stuffing can also be shaped into 3-inch balls (bake in 325°F. oven for 30 minutes) to be used as a garnish on the turkey platter.

Baked Filled Squash

This is the squash dish to prepare for "squash haters!" Even children ask for second helpings.

4 acorn squash, cut in half lengthwise	1 medium orange, peeled and chopped
salt	½ cup seedless raisins
1 cup tart apple, chopped	½ cup brown sugar
1 cup cranberries, chopped	2 tablespoons butter, melted

Preheat oven to 350°F.

Remove seeds from squash and place cut side down in baking dish. Bake in preheated 350°F. oven for 30 to 35 minutes. Turn cut side up and sprinkle each cavity with salt. Combine remaining ingredients and fill squash with fruit mixture. Return squash to oven and continue baking for 25 to 30 minutes, or until squash is tender.

Yield: 8 servings.

Cranberry Bread

 For an exciting brunch idea serve this American favorite with ginger marmalade. It is equally good for lunch with chicken salad.

2 cups flour
1½ teaspoons baking powder
½ teaspoon baking soda
1½ teaspoons salt
1 cup sugar
½ cup wheat germ
¼ cup butter or margarine, softened

1 egg, beaten
2 teaspoons grated orange rind
¾ cup orange juice
1 cup cranberries, coarsely chopped
½ cup pecans, chopped

Preheat oven to 350°F.

Sift together the flour, baking powder, baking soda, and salt. Add sugar and wheat germ. Add softened butter and mix well. Stir in beaten egg, orange rind, and juice. Fold in berries and pecans. Pour into greased 9-by-5-by-3-inch pan. Bake in preheated 350 °F. oven for 50 minutes, or until toothpick inserted in center comes out clean. Cool on wire rack.

Yield: 1 loaf.

Cranberry-Banana Bread

 Bananas make this a moist bread that is especially delicious the second or third day. Make several to freeze for busy days.

¹/₃ cup butter, softened

²/₃ cup granulated sugar

2 eggs, beaten

3 bananas, mashed

1¾ cups flour, sifted

2 teaspoons baking powder

¼ teaspoon baking soda

½ teaspoon salt

1½ cups fresh cranberries, ground and drained

1 cup walnuts, chopped

Preheat oven to 350 °F.

Cream together the butter and sugar. Add the eggs and beat well. Stir in the mashed bananas. Sift together the flour, baking powder, baking soda, and salt. Add the sifted dry ingredients to the banana mixture and stir well. Stir in the cranberries and chopped nuts. Turn into greased 9-by-5-by-3-inch loaf pan. Bake in preheated 350 °F oven for about 1 hour. Cool on wire rack for 15 minutes before removing from pan.

Yield: 1 loaf.

Cranberry Hermits

Fragrantly spicy, these fruited cookies are delicious with mugs of hot cinnamon cider. Make a double batch and store some in the freezer for surprise guests after football games.

2 cups raisins
½ cup rum
¼ cup butter, softened
½ cup brown sugar, packed
2 eggs
1½ cups flour
1½ teaspoons baking soda

½ teaspoon ground cinnamon
½ teaspoon allspice
¼ teaspoon ground cloves
¼ teaspoon ground nutmeg
1 cup cranberries, chopped
1 cup walnuts, chopped

Preheat oven to 325°F.

In a large bowl soak the raisins in rum for 1 hour. In another large bowl cream together the butter and brown sugar until the mixture is light and fluffy. Beat in the eggs. Sift together the flour, baking soda, and spices and add to the butter mixture. Stir in the cranberries, walnuts, and the raisins with their liquid. Drop the dough by teaspoonfuls onto buttered baking sheets and bake the cookies in a preheated 325 °F. oven for 12 to 15 minutes, or until they are firm. Allow the cookies to cool on racks.

Yield: 3½ dozen.

Cranberry Ice Cream

For a festive and impressive dessert, prepare a molded bombe of Cranberry Ice Cream filled with orange sherbet and garnished with Candied Cranberries. People will be asking you to cater parties!

2 cups cranberries, washed and picked over
1 cup fine granulated sugar

2 cups heavy cream
2 cups light cream
1 cup orange-flavored liqueur
¼ cup lemon juice

In a heavy saucepan combine the cranberries with sugar. Simmer the mixture, covered, over moderate heat for 15 minutes. Allow the mixture to cool slightly and then work it through a sieve into a bowl. Thoroughly mix in heavy and light creams, liqueur, and lemon juice. Pour the mixture into an ice-cream freezer and crank until the ice cream is thick. Place the ice cream in plastic containers and store in freezer.

Yield: 1 gallon.

Pink Peach Compote

If you use commercial cranberry sauce for this compote, you may want to reduce the amount of sugar you add. This is an excellent dessert for a dinner of standing rib roast.

1½ cups whole
  cranberry sauce

¼ cup sugar

1 tablespoon lemon
  juice

¼ cup ginger brandy

¼ teaspoon ground
  cinnamon

8 fresh peaches,
  skinned, pitted, and
  quartered

fresh mint

Preheat oven to 350°F.

In a medium saucepan combine cranberry sauce, sugar, lemon juice, brandy, and cinnamon. Bring mixture to a boil. Place the prepared peaches in a 1½-quart baking dish and pour cranberry mixture over fruit. Cover dish and bake in preheated 350°F. oven for 30 to 40 minutes, or until peaches are tender. Spoon warm fruit into sherbet glasses, garnish with fresh mint, and serve.

Yield: 6 servings.

Cranberry-Apple Pie

 Colorful, fragrant, and delicious! For a similar but quicker fall fruit combination, stuff large apples with a mixture of chopped cranberries, walnuts, brown sugar and spices, and bake.

2 cups fresh
  cranberries, ground
1 cup peeled apple,
  ground
½ cup raisins
½ cup orange pulp,
  ground
½ cup walnuts,
  chopped
1¼ cups sugar

2 tablespoons flour
½ teaspoon cinnamon
¼ teaspoon ground
  cloves
¼ teaspoon ground
  ginger
2 tablespoons butter
  pastry for 9-inch
  lattice pie

Preheat oven to 425 °F.

Combine cranberries, apple, raisins, orange, walnuts, sugar, flour, and spices in a bowl. Mix well. Turn into 9-inch pastry-lined pie plate. Dot with butter. Adjust lattice top and flute edges. Bake in a preheated 425°F. oven for 40 to 50 minutes, or until pastry is browned and juice begins to bubble through the lattice openings.

Yield: 6 to 8 servings.

Cranberries Jubilee

This spicy variation of the classic dessert is an impressive climax to any meal but it is my choice for a New Year's Eve dinner party.

2 cups cranberries, washed and picked over
1 cup sugar
¾ cup water
½ teaspoon cinnamon
¼ teaspoon ground cloves
¼ teaspoon ground nutmeg
½ teaspoon arrowroot
¼ cup peach-flavored brandy
vanilla ice cream

Prick each cranberry with a needle so the air can escape during cooking without bursting the skin of the fruit. Combine sugar and water in a saucepan, stirring to dissolve sugar. Bring to a boil and boil for 3 minutes. Add cranberries, cinnamon, cloves, and nutmeg. Bring the mixture to a boil, reduce heat, and simmer for 6 to 8 minutes, or until the berries are soft but still retain their shape. Mix the arrowroot with a little cold water and stir into cranberry mixture. Continue stirring until sauce thickens. Turn into blazer pan of chafing dish. Heat the peach-flavored brandy in a small pan, ignite the spirit, and pour over cranberry mixture. Serve the cranberries over vanilla ice cream at once.

Yield: 2 cups sauce.

Cranberry Conserve

This conserve is especially tasty with fowl, but adds a distinctive touch to any meal. The teen-age sons of a friend told me it was the greatest on cold turkey sandwiches, so I tried it. They were right!

4 cups cranberries	2½ cups sugar
1 unpeeled orange, finely chopped	1 cup seedless raisins
1½ cups water	½ cups walnuts, chopped

Combine the cranberries, orange, and water in a large Dutch oven. Cook rapidly for 20 minutes, or until orange peel is tender. Add sugar and raisins. Bring the mixture to a boil slowly, stirring frequently, until sugar dissolves. Reduce heat and simmer the mixture, stirring occasionally, for 15 to 20 minutes. Stir in walnuts the last 5 minutes of cooking. Ladle the hot conserve into hot, sterilized jars and process in hot water bath (see chapter 2).

Yield: 4 to 5 half-pints.

Classic Cranberry Sauce

What holiday meal is complete without this traditional sauce? When preparing it, be sure the berries cook only until they pop; cooked longer, they will turn bitter. Without canning, the sauce can safely be refrigerated for a week.

6 cups sugar
6 cups water
12 cups (3 pounds)
  cranberries, washed

Combine sugar and water in a 10-quart Dutch oven. Bring mixture to a boil over medium heat, stirring to dissolve sugar. Add the cranberries and cook until skins pop, about 5 minutes. Remove pot from heat and ladle hot sauce into hot, sterilized jars, leaving a ½-inch head space. Adjust lids and process in hot water bath for 5 minutes (see chapter 2).

Yield: 6 pints.

Cranberry Ketchup

 This is what our ancestors used before the commercial product was available! You will be impressed with the results.

4 pounds cranberries,
washed and picked
over

4 medium onions,
chopped

2½ cups water

2½ cups vinegar

1 teaspoon salt

2 teaspoons ground
cloves

2 teaspoons allspice

½ teaspoon mace

1 teaspoon paprika

In a large Dutch oven combine the cranberries, onions, and water. Bring the mixture to a boil and cook over moderate heat until the cranberries burst. Force the mixture through a sieve and return it to the Dutch oven. Add the remaining ingredients and bring the mixture to a boil. Reduce heat and simmer slowly, stirring occasionally, until mixture is thick. Pour the ketchup into hot, sterilized jars and seal with self-sealing lids.

Yield: 4 pints.

Cranberry Chutney

Do not keep this chutney just for the days when you serve curry. Put a dollop on cream cheese and crackers for cocktail nibbles.

4 cups cranberries

2 green apples, peeled, cored, and diced

1 orange, unpeeled, thinly sliced, and seeded

¼ cup chopped onion

½ cup seedless raisins

1½ cups brown sugar

1 cup cider vinegar

¼ teaspoon ground ginger

¼ teaspoon ground cloves

¼ teaspoon allspice

¼ teaspoon mustard seed

½ teaspoon curry powder

Combine all the ingredients in a large saucepan. Bring the mixture to a boil over medium heat. Reduce heat and simmer, uncovered, for 15 minutes, or until it is thickened, stirring frequently. Ladle the hot chutney into hot, sterilized jars and seal with self-sealing lids. Process in hot water bath for 10 minutes (see chapter 2). Store in a cool, dark place and allow chutney to age for 2 to 3 weeks before serving.

Yield: 5 half-pints.

Cranberry-Apple Wine

The pilgrim cranberry blends with the fruit of the Garden of Eden to produce a sinfully declicious rosé. The distinctive flavor improves stews, roasts, and game— whether you put the wine in the pot for cooking or in a glass for drinking!

10 cups (2½ pounds)
  cranberries,
  chopped
8 pounds apples,
  chopped
1 gallon boiling water
8 cups sugar

1 cup raisins,
  chopped
3 tablespoons citric
  acid (available in
  wine supply stores)
1 packet dry wine
  yeast

Place the chopped cranberries and apples in a 2-gallon crock and pour the boiling water over all. Allow the mixture to cool to room temperature. Stir in the sugar, chopped raisins, and citric acid. Sprinkle the dry yeast on the surface of the mixture. Cover the crock and store in a dark place for 1 week, pushing down the foam and floating fruit once a day. At the end of this period strain the mixture through a jelly bag into a clean 1-gallon bottle, leaving a 3-inch head space. Secure fermentation lock on mouth of bottle and allow to stand at room temperature, in a dark place, for 3 to 4 weeks, or until fermentation stops. Siphon the wine into a clean 1-gallon storage jar, adding a dry, red wine, if necessary, to completely fill jar. Store for 3 months at 50°F. to 55°F. Repeat this siphoning process twice more, at 3-month intervals. After the third racking, the wine is ready to be bottled.

Yield: 1 gallon.

Cranberry Cooler

 Refreshingly tart in flavor, this summer pink drink is a favorite prelude to beach house dinners. If you are entertaining guests, prepare a double recipe, because they always want refills.

2⅓ cups cranberry
  juice, chilled
1⅓ cups grapefruit
  juice, chilled

¾ cup gin
ice cubes
orange slices

In a large pitcher combine cranberry juice, grapefruit juice, and gin. Mix well. Add ice cubes and orange slices. Chill and serve.

Yield: 4 drinks.

Pink Cloud

 Thick and frothy, this is a variation of a drink we first tasted while vacationing in the Caribbean. Every time I prepare it, I think of lazy island afternoons and bright blue skies.

½ cup cranberry juice
  cocktail, chilled
2 ounces light rum
2 ounces Grenadine

2 ounces cherry-
  flavored brandy
1 banana
4 ice cubes
  fresh mint

Combine all the ingredients in a blender and mix thoroughly until the ice is finely chipped and the mixture smooth. Serve cold with a garnish of fresh mint.

Yield: 2 servings.

Cranberry Cordial

 If you start this in early fall, when the berries first appear in the market, the cordial will be ready for holiday guests.

4 cups cranberries,
  coarsely chopped
3 cups sugar
2 cups light rum

Place the chopped cranberries in a half-gallon jar that has a tightly fitting lid. Add sugar and rum. Adjust lid securely and store in a cool, dark place. Invert jar or stir every day for 6 weeks. Strain cordial into bottles and seal with corks.

Yield: 3¼ cups.

Spiced Cranberry Wine Punch

Hot punches are traditional after sleigh rides or caroling and this one justifies "braving the elements!" Be sure your serving bowl is warm before adding the punch.

1 4-inch cinnamon
stick

12 whole cloves

1 teaspoon whole
allspice

1 32-ounce bottle
cranberry juice
cocktail

1 6-ounce can frozen
orange juice
concentrate, thawed

2 cups water

½ cup sugar

peel of 1 orange, cut
in strips

6 cups dry red wine

orange slices

Tie cinnamon sticks, whole cloves, and allspice in cheesecloth bag. Combine cranberry juice, orange juice concentrate, water, sugar, and orange peel in saucepan. Add spice bag and bring mixture to a boil, stirring, over moderate heat. Reduce heat and simmer, uncovered, for 15 minutes. Add wine. Heat thoroughly, but do not boil. Remove spice bag. Pour punch into warm serving bowl and garnish with orange slices.

Yield: 20 to 25 servings.

Chapter Six
The Translucent Berries

$\mathcal{A}$s a child growing up in New York State, I frequently accompanied my father to the abandoned orchard where he indulged his hobby of keeping bees. Wearing the necessary protective headgear, he would swing the smoke canisters like a priest offering incense in church, while I explored the overgrown areas farthest away from the hives. The apples—untended, unsprayed, and bitter—were always a disappointment, but wild berries abounded, ripening at different times throughout the warm summer months. Blackcaps, mulberries, and wild strawberries were represented but the family favorites were the big greenish white gooseberries and the pearllike red currants. They were the delicacies that could not be purchased anywhere! The gooseberries, because of their generous size, and the currants, because they grew in large clusters, rapidly filled the berry pails. At home the berries were brewed and stewed into various treats that brightened and enhanced mealtime.

Currants, small, translucent berries with a pleasantly sour flavor, have been known since the middle of the fourteenth century. Native to northern Europe and Eurasia, they are red, white, or black when mature. Black currants were avoided, however, because of the belief that they bred worms in the human stomach. This myth may have evolved because of the primitive association between evil and dark colors. This fear was eventually overcome and all currants were then thought to possess therapeutic properties beneficial to gout, arthritis, dysentery, and various other complaints.

Currants seem to be appreciated more in Europe than in this country despite their early usage in the diet of native American Indians. Black currants are used in France to make a liqueur known as cassis, while the red and white varieties are made into a famous and expensive preserve called Bar-le-Duc.

Like grapes, currants have many natural wine yeast cells on the surface of the fruit, which led to the early development of currant wine. Possessing a fine flavor, the wine ages well and can be enjoyed as much as a century after the original bottling.

Although currants are used primarily in pies and jellies, their tartness makes them more adaptable to usage with meat than most other berries. Currant relishes and jellies have the versatility to enhance main courses of venison and ham as well as salads and cookies.

The packages of dried "currants" sold in stores are not real currants at all, but rather a small, special type of raisin. Fresh currants and the dried variety are not interchangeable in recipes and it should be noted which type is intended. All the recipes offered here call for either currant jelly or the fresh currants available in produce markets.

The currant bush, which is found growing along streams and wet woodlands throughout Canada and the northern United States, has three-to-five lobed leaves with elongated clusters of pale purple flowers. Harvesting the fruit in midsummer is a relatively simple task because there are no thorns and the average four-foot height of the bush eliminates the need to stoop.

Because currant bushes are hosts for a rust virus that attacks white pine trees, it is illegal in some states to plant them. Growers will ship only to states where permitted, but if you happen to live where currant bushes are legal, the cultivation of the plant is easy. In the North the plant requires a spring planting, while in milder areas it is better to plant in the fall. At planting, the tops of the bushes should be cut back and there should be an annual pruning of old, weak growth.

The gooseberry, a relative of currants, has the same translucent quality that allows the veins of the fruit to be seen through the skin. It is a distinctive berry with a small, brown "tail" opposite the stem, and can be red, green, yellow, or white, although the most common variety is yellowish white.

Hardy by nature, the gooseberry grows in Canada and the northern regions of the United States. Despite its availability in this country, the gooseberry has declined in popularity here in the last fifty years, as evidenced by the decreasing number of recipes to be found in contemporary cookbooks. In its native Europe—especially England—the gooseberry continues to be very much in demand.

The gooseberry may be the only fruit in history to have had fan clubs established in its honor. During the late eighteenth and early nineteenth centuries, gooseberry clubs were formed in the middle and northern sections of England. These clubs were organized to promote the cultivation of gooseberries, and laborers vied for prizes that were donated by local pub-owners. The size of the competing fruit was of great importance and the winning entries were often as large as plums.

The spiny gooseberry shrub has leaves that are almost round with five lobes. The bushes thrive in shady areas and produce sour, fleshy fruit that, depending on variety, is hairy or smooth.

Because gooseberry plants are also hosts for the rust virus, they are subject to the same legal restrictions that determine where currants may be cultivated. Gooseberries are good garden plants, however, for those people who live in areas where the shrubs are legal. They require little care and do not spread randomly the way many berry bushes do. The plants should be set four feet apart and need to be pruned in the early spring. New plants are easily started by bending a low branch over and burying it in the soil with the tip sticking out. Mulching the plants every summer ensures a good harvest, providing fruit for wine, pies, and preserves.

Hors-d'oeuvre Sausage Balls

 It is worth planning a party just so you can serve this appetizer. Prepare the meat days ahead and store in the freezer until party day. Thaw and warm the sausage balls in the oven before adding to the sauce in the chafing dish.

2 pounds bulk
    sausage
	½ teaspoon lemon
	    juice

1 cup currant jelly	½ cup sherry
1 cup Indian chutney	1 cup sour cream

Form sausage in small balls and cook over moderate heat in a skillet. In the top of a double boiler heat the currant jelly until melted. Stir in chutney, lemon juice, and sherry until well mixed. Remove from heat. Pour the mixture into a chafing dish and stir in sour cream. Add sausage balls and serve warm with toothpicks.

Yield: 12 to 15 servings.

Cream of Curried Currant Soup

 Serve this rich, subtle soup in colorful Oriental bowls and be prepared to share the recipe with your guests.

3 cups chicken stock
1 cup currant jelly
1 cup apple, freshly grated
1 cup onion, grated
2 stalks celery, grated
2 cloves
1 bay leaf
1 teaspoon curry powder

1 tablespoon cold milk
salt
cayenne pepper to taste
1/3 cup cooked rice
2 egg yolks
1/2 cup heavy cream
seasoning to taste
fresh parsley

Combine stock, jelly, apple, onion, celery, cloves, and bay leaf in a saucepan and simmer over moderate heat for 15 minutes. Stir in the curry powder mixed with cold milk, salt, cayenne pepper, and the cooked rice. Force the soup through a fine sieve into another saucepan. Bring the mixture to a boil. Beat egg yolks well and combine with heavy cream. Add the egg mixture to the soup, season to taste, and serve hot with fresh parsley.

Yield: 6 to 8 servings.

Iced Currant and Apple Soup

 This blending of currants and apples is a good reason why fruit soups are so popular in northern Europe where they originated.

4 cups red or black
  currants, stemmed
  and washed
½ lemon, sliced
1 2-inch stick
  cinnamon
2 cloves

½ cup brown sugar
2 cups plus 3
  tablespoons water
3 cups apple, grated
1 tablespoon
  cornstarch
½ cup yogurt

Slightly crush the currants in a medium saucepan. Add the lemon, spices, and sugar. Stir well and allow to stand for 30 minutes. Add 2 cups water and bring to a boil over moderate heat. Stir in grated apple and simmer, covered, for 10 to 15 minutes. Remove the mixture from heat. Work the soup through a sieve, discarding pulp, lemon, and spices. Return to heat and simmer gently for 3 minutes. Mix cornstarch with 3 tablespoons cold water and stir into soup. Return soup to heat and simmer for 2 minutes. Remove from heat. Refrigerate for several hours before serving with yogurt.

Yield: 4 to 6 servings.

Hot Curried Fruit

The sauce for this buffet bonus can be made in advance and refrigerated until you are ready to prepare the fruit. The flavor is especially good with roast beef.

1 pineapple, peeled, cored, and sliced

4 pears, peeled, cored, and sliced

5 large apples, peeled, cored, and sliced

2 cups fresh currants, stemmed and washed

$^1/_3$ cup butter

$^2/_3$ cup light brown sugar, firmly packed

3 teaspoons curry powder

Preheat oven to 300°F.

Beginning with the pineapple, arrange the prepared fruit in layers in a large 4-inch-deep baking dish. Melt butter in a small saucepan. Stir in sugar and curry powder. Mix well. Pour curry mixture over fruit and bake, uncovered, in a preheated 300°F. oven for 1¼ to 1½ hours. If fresh currants are not available, substitute 1 cup Bar-le-Duc preserves, adjusting brown sugar to taste.

Yield: 8 to 10 servings.

Avocado Ring

Serve this Avocado Ring as a cooling, rich salad alone, or for a spectacular luncheon entrée fill the center with fresh cooked shrimp.

1 3-ounce package lemon gelatin	3 tablespoons lemon juice
1 cup boiling water	1 teaspoon salt
¾ cup mayonnaise	1 cup avocado, mashed
½ cup currant jelly, melted and cooled	¾ cup heavy cream, whipped

Dissolve gelatin in boiling water and chill until partially set. In a bowl combine mayonnaise, currant jelly, lemon juice, and salt. Add to the partially set gelatin mixture and whip with beater until blended. Fold in avocado and whipped cream. Pour into mold and chill until firm.

Yield: 6 to 8 servings.

Ham Salad with Currant Jelly Mayonnaise

This is a terrific weekend standby when people might not eat on schedule. Have it ready and guests can help themselves.

2 cups cooked ham, cubed
½ cup celery, chopped
¼ cup onion, chopped fine
½ cup dill pickles, drained and chopped
2 egg yolks
½ teaspoon dry mustard
½ teaspoon salt
1 teaspoon wine vinegar
1 cup vegetable oil
¼ cup currant jelly, melted and cooled
½ tablespoon lemon juice
salad greens

Mix together ham, celery, onion, and pickles. In a bowl combine egg yolks, mustard, salt, and vinegar. Beat with an electric mixer and add ¼ cup vegetable oil, drop by drop, until mixture begins to thicken. Add remaining oil in a fine stream, while beating. Add melted jelly and lemon juice. Combine currant jelly mayonnaise with ham mixture and serve on salad greens.

Yield: 6 servings.

Currant Sweet Potatoes with Apples

 For variety, patty pan squash—a white summer squash—can be substituted for potatoes in this cold weather vegetable dish.

4 medium sweet potatoes	¼ cup granulated sugar
3 apples	½ cup brown sugar
2 tablespoons butter	1 teaspoon ground nutmeg
½ cup currant jelly	

Boil the potatoes in their jackets in a saucepan until slightly tender, but not well done. When cool, peel and slice. Peel and thinly slice the apples. Layer the sliced potatoes and apples in a well-greased 2-quart casserole. In a small saucepan melt the butter and currant jelly, stirring until mixed. Stir in sugar and ground nutmeg. Pour the mixture over the potatoes and apples. Cover and bake in a preheated 350 °F oven for 1 hour. Uncover and place under broiler for 2 to 3 minutes before serving.

Yield: 6 to 8 servings.

Sauced Beets

 A colorful vegetable dish guaranteed to brighten any meal.

1 cup currant jelly	1 pound beets, cooked, peeled, and sliced
1 tablespoon cornstarch	
dash of salt	½ teaspoon grated lemon peel

Melt the currant jelly in a saucepan over moderate heat. Add the cornstarch and salt. Cook, stirring constantly, until the mixture is thick and bubbly. Add the sliced beets and grated lemon peel. Simmer, uncovered, for 10 minutes.

Yield: 6 to 8 servings.

Crazy Carrots

 This is the best way yet of convincing children to eat carrots! The crunchy texture of the Spiced Fresh Currants makes this a "second helping" vegetable.

6–8 medium carrots, peeled and thinly sliced	1–2 tablespoons butter
	¾ cup Spiced Fresh Currants (page 129)
water	
salt	

Combine the carrots, water, and salt in a saucepan. Cook, covered, for 15 minutes, or until almost tender. Drain water from saucepan. Add the butter and Spiced Fresh Currants to the carrots. Simmer the mixture, stirring, over low heat until the carrots are well coated.

Yield: 4 to 6 servings.

Roast Leg of Lamb with Wine

 An elegant main course recipe that was given to me by a California friend.

1 5–6-pound leg of lamb

1 garlic clove, crushed

3 tablespoons lemon juice

¼ teaspoon curry powder

¼ teaspoon ground ginger

¼ teaspoon dry mustard

salt and pepper

4 tablespoons currant jelly

1 cup Currant-Plum Wine (page 138) or any red wine

Wipe meat with a damp cloth. Do not remove paperlike covering of meat. Rub meat with crushed garlic and spread evenly with lemon juice. Combine curry powder, ground ginger, and dry mustard. Rub spices evenly over meat and cover with tinfoil. Refrigerate overnight. When ready to cook, season meat with salt and pepper. Roast, uncovered, in a preheated 325 °F oven for 30 to 35 minutes per pound. Combine jelly and wine. Remove roast from oven about 45 minutes before meat is done. Drain off excess fat. Return roast to pan, brush thoroughly with jelly-wine mixture, and return to oven. Brush meat with glaze mixture another three times before lamb is ready to be served.

Yield: 8 to 10 servings.

Mackerel with Gooseberry Sauce

A favorite dish in coastal Canada where mackerel is abundant.

6 mackerel fillets (½ pound each)
flour
salt and pepper
butter

Dredge the fillets in flour seasoned with salt and pepper. Sauté the fillets in butter, in a skillet, for 3 to 4 minutes on each side, or until they flake easily when tested with a fork. Serve hot with Gooseberry Sauce.

Gooseberry Sauce

4 cups gooseberries, stemmed, tailed, and washed
½ cup water

½ cup sugar
¼ teaspoon ground nutmeg
pinch of salt

Cook the gooseberries, water, and sugar in a saucepan over moderate heat until the mixture comes to a boil. Reduce heat and simmer for 15 to 20 minutes, or until the berries are soft. Remove from heat and work the mixture through a sieve. Stir nutmeg, salt, and additional sugar, if desired, into purée. Reheat sauce and serve with mackerel fillets.

Yield: 6 servings.

Currant Glazed Ham

 Everyone, it seems, has a favorite recipe for ham glaze. This is mine.

1 10–12-pound bone-
  in ham
  whole cloves
  glaze
1½ cups currant jelly

¼ cup Dijon mustard
¼ teaspoon ground
  allspice
½ cup golden raisins

Preheat oven to 325°F.

Place ham, fat side up, in shallow roasting pan. Score fat in diamond pattern and stud with cloves. Insert meat thermometer, being sure that it does not touch bone. Bake the ham in a preheated 325°F. oven for 2 to 2½ hours, or until thermometer registers 130°.

Yield: 12 to 14 servings.

Glaze

In a saucepan stir together the currant jelly and mustard until well combined. Add allspice and raisins. Simmer, uncovered, over low heat for 10 minutes. Baste the ham with the currant glaze 3 or 4 times during the last 30 minutes of baking.

Yield: approximately 2 cups.

Roast Venison

Venison is not the type of meat you can readily buy, but if you have a successful hunter in the family, this is a delicious way to serve the loin.

1 8–10-pound venison loin roast

3 onions, sliced

2 carrots, sliced

3 celery stalks, finely diced

2 bay leaves, crushed

1 teaspoon thyme

1 teaspoon black pepper

1 cup water

1$\frac{1}{3}$ cups vinegar

1½ cups red wine (preferably a currant wine)

Wash and rub clean the roast and place in an earthen container. Combine the remaining ingredients and pour over meat. Cover the container and allow meat to stand in marinade, in refrigerator, for at least 12 hours, turning occasionally.

Seasoning

   2 garlic cloves, cut in
      slivers
   1 teaspoon salt

Preheat oven to 325°F.

When ready for roasting, remove meat from refrigerator and wipe with paper towels. Do not wash. Insert garlic slivers, sprinkle with salt, and place in roasting pan. Roast, uncovered, in preheated 325°F. oven, basting frequently with marinade and pan drippings, until meat thermometer registers "done lamb."

Pan Sauce

   1 cup currant jelly
   1 tablespoon brandy
   ½ cup heavy cream

Remove meat from pan when cooked and keep warm on serving platter in oven. Stir currant jelly, brandy, and heavy cream into meat drippings in roasting pan. Cook, over moderate heat, stirring, until the mixture thickens. Serve sauce over sliced venison.

Yield: 10 to 12 servings.

Nutty Red Currant Muffins

Fragrant and spicy, these muffins are good anytime. They freeze well, so they can be made ahead and reheated in foil.

2 cups all-purpose flour, sifted

¾ cup plus 2 tablespoons sugar

3 teaspoons baking powder

1 teaspoon salt

1 teaspoon ground cinnamon

¼ teaspoon ground nutmeg

½ cup pecans, chopped

2 eggs, well beaten

²/₃ cup milk

¹/₃ cup cooking oil

1¼ cups fresh red currants, stemmed and washed

Preheat oven to 375°F.

Sift together flour, ¾ cup sugar, baking powder, salt, ¾ teaspoon ground cinnamon, and nutmeg. Stir in chopped pecans and set aside. Combine beaten eggs, milk, and cooking oil. Add egg mixture to dry ingredients. Stir just until moistened. Spoon a generous layer of batter into 18 greased muffin cups. Scatter a layer of fresh currants in each cup and fill with remaining batter. In a small dish combine 2 tablespoons sugar with ¼ teaspoon ground cinnamon. Sprinkle tops of muffins with cinnamon mixture and bake in a preheated 375°F oven for 20 to 25 minutes, or until the muffins are golden.

Yield: 1½ dozen.

Currant Jelly Cookies

My personal nomination for best cookie. The last time I made them, they didn't even last until supper!

½ cup butter,
  softened

¼ cup light brown
  sugar, firmly packed

1 egg, lightly beaten

½ teaspoon almond
  extract

1¼ cups flour, sifted

¼ cup ground
  almonds

⅓ cup currant jelly

Preheat oven to 375°F.

In a medium bowl beat the softened butter and brown sugar with a spoon until smooth. Blend in the egg and almond extract. Stir in flour, just until combined. Mix in ground almonds. Refrigerate batter for 30 minutes. Roll the chilled dough into balls 1 inch in diameter. Place the cookies 2 inches apart on an ungreased cookie sheet. Make a depression in the center of each cookie with thumb. Bake in a preheated 375°F. oven for 10 to 12 minutes, or until a delicate golden brown. Cool on wire rack. Fill each depression with currant jelly.

Yield: 2 dozen.

Pumpkin-Red Currant Bread

 If red currants are not available, you can substitute fresh cranberries in this spicy recipe. This can be frozen for several months or wrapped and stored in the refrigerator for 4 to 6 days.

⅓ cup butter

1⅓ cups brown sugar, firmly packed

2 eggs

1 cup cooked pumpkin

1⅔ cups flour

¼ teaspoon baking powder

1 teaspoon baking soda

½ teaspoon salt

½ teaspoon ground nutmeg

½ teaspoon ground cinnamon

½ teaspoon ground cloves

⅓ cup water

1 cup red currants, stemmed and washed

½ cup walnuts, chopped

Preheat oven to 350°F.

Cream together butter and sugar. Add eggs, one at a time, beating thoroughly after each addition. Stir in cooked pumpkin. Sift together flour, baking powder, baking soda, salt, nutmeg, cinnamon, and cloves. Add alternately with water to the butter mixture. Stir in fresh currants and chopped nuts. Pour batter into greased 9-by-5-by-3-inch loaf pan. Bake in a preheated 350°F. oven for 30 to 40 minutes, or until cake tester comes out clean. Turn out on rack to cool.

Yield: 1 loaf.

Spiced Fresh Currants

 This is one of the best berry relishes you can make! It is delicious as an accompaniment with meat, as a roast glaze, and on crackers and cheese.

2¼ quarts red currants, stemmed and washed

1 teaspoon ground cinnamon

1 teaspoon ground cloves

¼ teaspoon ground allspice

¼ cup cider vinegar

¼ cup water

7¼ cups sugar

½ bottle liquid fruit pectin

In a large saucepan combine the currants, spices, vinegar, and water. Bring to a boil, stirring constantly. Reduce heat and simmer, covered, for 10 minutes. Measure 4 cups of the currant mixture into a large Dutch oven. Add sugar and mix thoroughly. Bring the mixture to a full rolling boil over high heat and boil hard for 1 minute, stirring constantly. Remove from heat and immediately stir in liquid pectin. Stir and skim for 5 minutes. Quickly ladle the mixture into hot, sterilized jars, leaving a ½-inch head space. Adjust lids and process in boiling water bath for 5 minutes (see chapter 2).

Yield: 6 to 8 half-pints.

Fresh Currant Pie

Full of flavor and beautiful to look at, this blending of almonds and currants is sure to become a family favorite.

pastry for 1 9-inch,
2-crust pie

½ cup almonds,
chopped and
blanched

3 cups currants,
stemmed and
washed

1½ cups sugar

½ teaspoon salt

½ teaspoon almond
extract

4 tablespoons quick-
cooking tapioca

1 tablespoon butter or
margarine

Preheat oven to 450°F.

Line a 9-inch pie pan with pastry crust. Spread chopped almonds in the pastry shell. Place the currants in a bowl and crush lightly with a spoon. Stir in the sugar, salt, almond extract, and tapioca. Stir gently to mix and turn into pastry shell. Dot with butter. Adjust top crust, flute edges to seal, and cut vents. Bake the pie in a preheated 450°F. oven for 10 minutes. Reduce heat to 350°F. and bake for 30 minutes, or until crust is golden and the juices are bubbly.

Yield: 6 to 8 servings.

Gooseberry Pie

 Gooseberry pie is a treat that causes many people to become nostalgic about "the good old days" when this was a summer staple of every cook's repertoire. Make several pies when the fruit is ripe and freeze them for baking on a winter afternoon.

4 cups gooseberries, stemmed, tailed, and washed

2 cups sugar

3 tablespoons quick-cooking tapioca

½ teaspoon cinnamon

¼ teaspoon salt

grated rind of 1 lemon

pastry for 1 9-inch, 2-crust pie

1 tablespoon butter

milk

sugar

Preheat oven to 450°F.

In a medium bowl combine the berries, sugar, tapioca, cinnamon, salt, and lemon rind. Toss well, slightly mashing some of the berries. Spoon the gooseberry mixture into the pie shell and dot with butter. Adjust top crust, crimping the edges to seal. Cut a small air vent in the center of the crust and make several small slits around the vent. Brush crust with milk and sprinkle with sugar. Bake the pie in a preheated 450°F. oven for 10 minutes. Reduce the temperature to 350°F. and continue baking for 40 to 50 minutes, or until crust is golden. Allow pie to cool slightly on a rack before serving.

Yield: 6 to 8 servings.

Gooseberry Fool

This fragile blending of tart and sweet flavors is a classic English dessert.

1 quart gooseberries, tailed and washed
¼ cup water
1 cup sugar
1 cup heavy cream

3 tablespoons powdered sugar
freshly grated nutmeg

In a heavy saucepan crush the berries slightly and stir in water and sugar. Simmer the berries over low heat, uncovered, for 10 to 15 minutes, or until tender. Work the berries through a sieve and add more sugar to the purée if needed. Allow the purée to cool. Whip the heavy cream with the powdered sugar until stiff peaks form. Gently fold the cream into the purée, spoon into sherbet glasses, and sprinkle with grated nutmeg.

Yield: 6 servings.

Red Currant Mousse

An unusual, impressive dessert that is perfect for a buffet dinner.

2½ cups red currants, stemmed and washed
1 cup water
1 cup sugar
1 envelope unflavored gelatin

½ teaspoon salt
1 cup milk
1 teaspoon vanilla
2 cups heavy cream, whipped

Combine the currants with water and cook over moderate heat until the mixture comes to a boil. Remove from heat and work the fruit through a sieve. Set the purée aside. Thoroughly mix sugar, gelatin, and salt in a small saucepan. Add milk and stir over moderate heat until gelatin and sugar dissolve. Remove from heat and chill until partially set. Add vanilla. Fold in fruit purée and whipped cream. Spoon into 1½-quart soufflé dish and chill for at least 4 to 5 hours until firm. Serve with Raspberry-Currant Sauce.

Yield: 6 to 8 servings.

Raspberry-Currant Sauce

 A versatile sauce to be used on puddings and ice creams, as well as Red Currant Mousse.

2 cups fresh
  raspberries, washed
¼ cup sugar
½ cup red currant
  jelly
1 tablespoon
  cornstarch

Crush raspberries in a small saucepan. Add sugar and heat, stirring frequently, until mixture comes to a boil. Strain. Add currant jelly and heat, stirring, until jelly is melted and well blended. Mix the cornstarch with 2 tablespoons cooled raspberry-currant juice. Heat the remaining juice to a boil, stir in cornstarch, and cook, stirring, until thickened. Chill before serving.

Yield: 6 to 8 servings.

Red Currant Jelly

*Currant jelly—whether homemade or commercial—
should be in every kitchen because it is a wonderful
addition to countless recipes. Pretty jars of this
shimmering red jelly can be tied with festive plaid
ribbons for thoughtful holiday giving.*

3 quarts ripe currants,
   stemmed and
   washed
1 cup water
7 cups sugar
½ bottle liquid fruit
   pectin

Crush fully ripe currants in a large saucepan. Add water and bring to a boil over moderate heat. Reduce heat
and simmer, covered, for 10 minutes. Place fruit in jelly
bag and squeeze out juice. Measure 5 cups juice into a
large Dutch oven and thoroughly stir in sugar. Bring
the mixture to a boil over high heat, stirring constantly.
Stir in liquid pectin and bring to a full rolling boil.
Stirring, boil hard for 1 minute. Remove from heat.
Alternately stir and skim off foam. Pour the jelly into
hot, sterilized jars, leaving a ½-inch head space. Seal at
once with melted paraffin.

Yield: approximately 7 half-pints.

Gooseberry Relish

This is a variation of a recipe that goes back to pioneer days; it is especially interesting with smoked meat or fish.

6 cups gooseberries, tailed and washed	1½ teaspoons ground ginger
2 medium onions	1½ teaspoons salt
1½ cups seedless raisins	½ teaspoon cayenne pepper
2 cups light brown sugar, firmly packed	1 quart white wine vinegar
1 tablespoon dry mustard	

Coarsely chop the gooseberries and onions. Combine the gooseberries, onions, and remaining ingredients in a large Dutch oven. Cook the mixture over low heat, stirring frequently, for 1½ to 2 hours, or until it is thickened. Ladle the relish into hot, sterilized jars and adjust the lids securely. Allow the relish to mellow for several weeks.

Yield: 6 half-pints.

Black Currant Liqueur

 This can be your version of the French currant liqueur—cassis. For an easy dessert, swirl some of the liqueur through softened peach or vanilla ice cream and refreeze. Serve the "improved" ice cream in stemmed glasses with an additional splash of liqueur.

4 cups black currants,
    stemmed and
    washed
8 cloves

1 2-inch stick
    cinnamon
¾ cup sugar
2 cups gin

Crush the black currants and place in a large bowl with the cloves and cinnamon stick. Stir in sugar. Add gin and mix well until all the ingredients are well blended. Pour the mixture into a clean gallon jar and cork it tightly. Store the jar in a warm place for 40 days. Strain the liquid through cheesecloth into a clean container. Squeeze out the pulp in the cloth to extract as much liquid as possible. Pour the liqueur into a sterilized and dried quart bottle. Cork the bottle and set aside in a cool, dry, dark place for at least 1 week before serving.

Yield: 4 to 5 cups.

Currant-Plum Wine

This is a rich, full-bodied wine that is especially complementary to venison.

1 quart red currants, stemmed and washed

1 quart plums, pitted and washed

½ cup raisins, chopped

1 gallon boiling water

2 pounds sugar

1 Campden tablet, crushed

1 teaspoon pectic enzyme

½ teaspoon yeast nutrient

1 package quick-starting wine yeast

In a clean 2-gallon crock crush the currants and plums. Add the chopped raisins. Pour boiling water over the fruit and allow the mixture to cool to room temperature. Stir in sugar, crushed Campden tablet, and pectic enzyme. Cover the crock with plastic wrap and store, at room temperature, in a dark place for 1 day. On the second day stir in yeast nutrient and wine yeast. Cover crock again and ferment for 5 days, pushing down floating fruit twice daily. On the sixth day strain the mixture through a jelly bag, squeezing, to extract all the juice. Pour juice into a 1-gallon jug, leaving a 4-inch head space. Adjust water lock on jug. Store wine, at room temperature, in a dark place for 2 to 4 weeks, or until fermentation completely ceases. Siphon the wine into a clean storage jug, filling completely. Store at 55°F. for 3 months. Repeat siphoning process twice more at 3-month intervals. Bottle wine during the ninth month. Allow wine to mature for 1 year before serving.

Yield: 1 gallon.

Mulled Currant Wine

The perfect warm-up after chopping down your own Christmas tree!

1 cup sugar
½ cup water
2 3-inch sticks cinnamon
½ lemon, thinly sliced
24 cloves

1 cup fresh lemon juice
3 cups pineapple juice
1 quart Currant-Plum Wine (page 138)
lemon slices
cinnamon sticks

Boil together the sugar, water, cinnamon sticks, lemon slices, and cloves for 5 minutes, or until thickened. Strain the syrup into a large saucepan. Add the lemon juice, pineapple juice, and Currant-Plum Wine. Heat the mixture thoroughly, but do not boil. Serve very hot, garnished with fresh lemon slices and cinnamon sticks.

Yield: 2 quarts.

Gooseberry Wine

Patience is the secret of fine gooseberry wine; allow the wine to age sufficiently before trying it.

4 quarts gooseberries,
   stemmed, tailed,
   and washed
3 quarts cold water
4 pounds sugar

1 package quick-
   starting wine yeast
½ teaspoon
   unflavored gelatin

In a clean 2-gallon crock crush the berries. Pour water over the fruit and stir until well mixed. Strain through jelly bag, squeezing to extract all the juice. Add sugar and stir to dissolve. Add the yeast. Cover the crock with plastic wrap and store, at room temperature, in a dark place for 5 days, pressing down the floating fruit twice daily. On the sixth day siphon into a clean 1-gallon jug, leaving a 4-inch head space. Attach water lock and allow to stand at room temperature for 1 month, or until fermentation ceases. Siphon wine into a clean 1-gallon jug, adding ½ teaspoon unflavored gelatin before sealing with cork. Siphon twice more, at 3-month intervals. Bottle wine at the end of the ninth month. This wine is best when allowed to mature for 1 to 2 years.

Yield: 1 gallon.

Chapter Seven
The Mysterious Raspberry

Although berry bushes commonly grow in remote, out-of-the-way areas of the countryside, offering their crops to birds and other wildlife, raspberries and blackcaps seem to thrive in more unusual and accessible surroundings. Bordering shopping center parking lots and abandoned cemeteries, they yield plump harvests that go unnoticed and uneaten. The irony is that people rush past the "free food" to buy raspberries in the market—if there's any for sale—at ninety-nine cents a half-pint.

It was the thick raspberry patches we found growing in such strange places that taught us to carry lightweight containers in the car during the summer months. Children's plastic sand pails or empty coffee cans with rope handles can be stored in the car trunk in early May and used throughout the berry season. These same pails, incidentally, can be carried into the golden days of autumn for the gathering of nuts.

Raspberries, possibly the sweetest and most delicately flavored of the edible berries, appear to have escaped any real notice until the nineteenth century. It is thought, based on evidence supplied by fossils found in Swiss lake dwellings, that the raspberry may have been known some centuries before Christ, yet there are no references to *Rubus idaeus* in ancient Latin, Greek,

141

or Oriental writings. Cultivation of the berry, which is native to most temperate regions of the world, occurred as early as the mid-sixteenth century in England, where it was also known as hindberry. The sketchy references available indicate that the taste of the raspberry was considerably improved by breeding and cultivation, which may explain why generations of people ignored the fruit as a source of food.

Native American Indians valued the berries and used them to make cooling drinks and to press into dried cakes for winter meals. The fruit, leaves, and roots, thought to have healing properties, were variously made into poultices for wounds and drinks to ease dysentery and sore throats. Pregnant women were urged to drink raspberry-leaf tea to avoid miscarriage and improve their general well-being. Raspberries are high in vitamin content, having proportionately the same amount as oranges. Because they are also very rich in pectin, they are one of the best fruits for preserving.

Growing wild throughout Europe and North America, the berry, composed of numerous round drupelets, falls easily from the central core that supports it until ripe. Birds, eating the fleshy fruit, carry the seeds contained in the drupelets, and randomly scatter them over the countryside. Once established, the plants propagate themselves by sending up new, finely prickled canes, two to five feet tall. Those who hope to harvest the fruit can easily identify the wild plants by the serrated leaflets. Long before the white blossoms appear, raspberry patches can be located when spring breezes reveal the distinctive whitish, downy underside of the foliage. The observant harvester can return—hopefully before the hungry birds—in July and August to gather the soft, ripe fruit.

Because the popular berries are sold at roadside stands as quickly as they can be picked, home cultivation seems to be the only way to ensure availability of the fruit. The plants, although easy to grow, need to be pruned and controlled in the garden before they run wild and yield smaller harvests. Each cane dies after producing fruit in its second year, and must be cut away. New shoots develop from the mother plant and repeat the cycle of bearing fruit and waning.

Because raspberries, like most fruit, require full sunlight, they are most successful when planted in an area free of shade. The plants should be set three to four feet apart, with six feet between rows. In the northern regions of the country the plants should be set in humus-enriched ground in the spring, while autumn planting is recommended for milder climates.

While there are white, yellow, and purple raspberries, the most common varieties are red and black. The black raspberry, also called blackcap or thimbleberry, is the "wild sister" found growing along creeks and hedgerows in the country. Blackcaps, although somewhat smaller than the red variety, can be used in any recipe that requires raspberries.

A very special addition to a winter meal is classic Blackcap Pie (page 160). Make it in July, store it in your home freezer, and bake it on a snowy December afternoon. The sweet aroma and taste will convince you, for a short time, that the locusts are humming and the sun is warm on your back.

Raspberry-Stuffed Baked Pears

Crushed macaroons added to the stuffing of this elegant appetizer give it a different taste. Be careful to cook the pears only until tender so they will retain their shape.

3 cups raspberries	6 firm, ripe pears with stems
½ cup walnuts, chopped	grated rind and juice of 1 lemon
1 cup sugar	kirsch

Preheat oven to 300°F.

Sprinkle 1 cup berries and walnuts with ⅓ cup sugar. Toss gently and set aside. Peel pears carefully, leaving stems attached. Core each pear from the bottom. Spoon sweetened berries and nuts into each cavity and place stuffed pears on their sides in a 10-by-6-by-2-inch baking dish. Sprinkle pears with grated lemon rind and juice. Crush 2 cups raspberries and press through a fine sieve. Stir in ⅔ cup sugar and kirsch to taste. Pour over pears. Bake in a preheated 300°F oven for 40 minutes, or until pears are tender. Turn pears occasionally and baste with juice. Spoon pears and juice into 6 long-stemmed glasses and serve warm as an appetizer.

Yield: 6 servings.

Soused Raspberries and Pineapple

Serve this in pineapple shells and give your table a gala appearance that will be the beginning of a luau. Add to the theme by arranging a tropical fruit centerpiece and serving Cherry-Berry Chicken as the entrée.

2 ripe pineapples
²/₃ cup fine sugar
¾ cup orange juice, freshly squeezed
¼ cup any orange-flavored liqueur

2 cups raspberries, washed
²/₃ cup kirsch
¹/₃ cup toasted almonds

With a sharp knife cut the pineapples and stems in half lengthwise. Remove and discard the cores and less tender pulp. Scoop out the remaining pulp and spoon into a bowl. Sprinkle with ¹/₃ cup fine sugar. Pour orange juice and orange-flavored liqueur over the pineapple, toss gently, and refrigerate for 2 hours, stirring occasionally. Put raspberries in another bowl, sprinkle with remaining fine sugar, and add kirsch. Toss and refrigerate for 2 hours, stirring occasionally. When ready to serve, spoon pineapple and berries into pineapple shells and garnish with toasted almonds.

Yield: 4 servings.

Ribbon Compote with Sabayon Sauce

One of the best ways to serve any fruit combination—fresh with a delicate sauce to complement the flavors.

2 oranges, peeled
1 pint blueberries, washed
2 peaches, peeled, pitted, and sliced

1 honeydew melon, seeded and cubed
1 pint raspberries, washed

Remove membranes from oranges and slice crosswise. Layer the slices in a very large brandy snifter or crystal bowl. Arrange the remaining fruit in order. Serve as an appetizer with Sabayon Sauce.

Sabayon Sauce

2 egg yolks
¼ cup sugar
¼ cup strawberry juice

¼ cup dry white wine
1 teaspoon grated lemon rind

Beat egg yolks and sugar in a medium bowl until the mixture ribbons when the beater is lifted. Stir in the remaining ingredients and transfer the mixture to the top of a double boiler. Whisk the mixture, over simmering water, for 10 minutes, or until the sauce is thick and triple in volume. Pour warm sauce over Ribbon Compote.

Yield: 4 to 6 servings.

Chilled Raspberry Soup

 This creamy pink soup with a sprig of green mint is as refreshing to look at as it is to eat. For a luxurious picnic in the country, serve it in white bowls as a prelude to a luncheon of cold salmon and wine.

4 cups fresh
   raspberries, washed
½ cup sugar
1 cup sour cream

1 cup cold water
1 cup dry white wine,
   chilled
fresh mint

Blend the raspberries in an electric blender until smooth. Combine the blended berries thoroughly with sugar and sour cream. Stir in water and wine. Chill the soup and serve cold garnished with mint sprigs.

Yield: 4 to 6 servings.

Raspberry-Cherry Soup

Fortunately, raspberries and cherries are in season simultaneously, so it is possible to enjoy this tasty combination.

2 cups raspberries, washed

2 cups sweet cherries, pitted

1½ quarts plus 2 tablespoons water

1 2-inch stick cinnamon

1 lemon, thinly sliced

½ cup sugar

2 cups rosé

1½ tablespoons cornstarch

½ cup almonds, finely ground

Crush the raspberries. Work them through a fine sieve into a large saucepan and set aside. Combine the cherries and 1½ quarts water in another saucepan. Simmer over moderate heat until the fruit is tender. Drain cherry liquid into raspberry purée. Work the cooked cherries through a fine sieve into the raspberry purée. Add cinnamon stick, lemon slices, sugar, and rosé. Simmer, stirring, for 3 minutes, or until sugar is dissolved. Dilute cornstarch with 2 tablespoons water and stir into soup. Simmer, stirring, until soup thickens. Remove cinnamon stick. Serve soup warm with a generous sprinkle of ground almonds.

Yield: 8 servings.

Melon Cups with Orange-Pecan Dressing

Prepare this southern-type dressing several hours in advance so the flavors can be thoroughly blended. By using a different flavored liqueur, you can invent a new dressing every week.

3 cantaloupe melons, halved and seeded

1½ pints fresh raspberries, washed

1 cup sour cream

½ cup powdered sugar, sifted

2 tablespoons orange juice

2 tablespoons orange-flavored liqueur

½ cup toasted pecans, finely chopped

Cut a thin slice from the bottom of each melon half so it will stand. Scoop pulp out of the melons and toss lightly with the raspberries. Spoon fruit into melon cups and store in refrigerator until ready to serve. Combine sour cream and powdered sugar in a bowl. Stir in orange juice and orange-flavored liqueur. Blend well. Fold in chopped pecans. Chill before serving with melon cups.

Yield: 6 servings.

Frozen Raspberry Salad

Sweet and creamy with the crunch of nuts, this delicate pink salad can be made the day ahead and stored in the freezer until your guests arrive. For the best results, allow it to stand at room temperature for 10 to 15 minutes before serving.

2 cups fresh
  raspberries
1 6-ounce package
  miniature
  marshmallows
2 3-ounce packages
  cream cheese,
  softened

$^2/_3$ cup mayonnaise
1 cup heavy cream,
  whipped
$^1/_4$ cup walnuts,
  chopped
  salad greens
  whole raspberries

Crush the raspberries in the top of a double boiler. Add marshmallows and heat, over water, until marshmallows are melted. Cool. Thoroughly blend softened cream cheese and mayonnaise. Add to the raspberry mixture. Fold in whipped cream and nuts. Spoon mixture into 10-by-6-by-2-inch dish and place in freezer for 3 to 4 hours. Cut into squares and serve on plates lined with salad greens. Garnish with whole raspberries.

Yield: 8 to 10 servings.

Fruited Wine Salad

Fresh fruits suspended like floating jewels in a sangria-type salad make this a colorful—and delicious— "make-ahead dish" for a summer party.

2 tablespoons
 unflavored gelatin
½ cup sugar
¼ teaspoon salt
2½ cups boiling water
½ cup burgundy
2 tablespoons fresh
 lemon juice
1 cup fresh

raspberries, washed
½ cup seedless green
 grapes, halved
1 cup mandarin
 oranges, drained
1 banana, thinly
 sliced
sour cream

Dissolve gelatin, sugar, and salt in boiling water. Stir in burgundy and lemon juice. Cool. When mixture begins to thicken, stir in fruit. Pour into a 1½-quart mold and refrigerate until firm. Serve with garnish of sour cream.

Yield: 8 to 10 servings.

Cherry-Berry Chicken

This hearty, Oriental-type chicken is especially satisfying with curried rice or steamed white rice and Chinese pea pods with mushrooms. To accentuate the food I like to serve it on Imari plates with a very simple centerpiece on the table.

1 2–3-pound chicken, cut up	2 tablespoons grated orange peel
⅓ cup flour	½ cup orange juice
1 teaspoon salt	¼ teaspoon ground ginger
¼ cup butter or margarine	
1½ cups Raspberry-Cherry Conserve* (page 163)	

Preheat oven to 350 °F.

Coat chicken pieces with flour and salt mixture. Heat butter in skillet and brown chicken on all sides. Place chicken in shallow baking dish and bake, uncovered, in a preheated 350°F. oven for 30 minutes. In a small bowl combine the conserve, orange peel, juice, and ground ginger. Baste chicken with the conserve mixture and bake for an additional 30 minutes, basting frequently. Arrange chicken on a warm platter.

Yield: 4 to 6 servings.

* If you have no conserve on hand, you may substitute ½ cup raspberry jam and 1 cup pitted sweet cherries, blended with ⅛ teaspoon almond extract and ¼ cup blanched almonds. The sweetness may be reduced to suit your taste by adding a teaspoon of lemon juice.

Sherried Sweet Potatoes

Gone are the days of dull vegetables! This is a delicious version of baked sweet potatoes.

6 medium-sized sweet potatoes, boiled until tender

2 tablespoons butter

2 cups pineapple, cut in chunks

¾ cup Raspberry-Cherry Conserve (page 163)

½ cup sherry

⅛ teaspoon salt

½ teaspoon nutmeg

½ cup raisins

½ cup almonds, blanched and slivered

Preheat oven to 350°F.

Slice the tender sweet potatoes into ½-inch thick slices. Place a single layer of potatoes in a buttered casserole. Spread with a thin topping of pineapple chunks. Repeat layers. In a small saucepan combine Raspberry-Cherry Conserve, sherry, salt, and nutmeg. Heat, stirring, until conserve is melted and mixture is blended. Pour over potatoes. Sprinkle with raisins and almonds. Bake in a preheated 350°F. oven for 1 hour. Serve with Cranberry-Stuffed Pork Crown Roast (page 88).

Yield: 4 to 6 servings.

Raspberry Jam Cookies

These old-fashioned cookies that bring back childhood memories of good aromas and after-school snacks can be made ahead and frozen for a month.

½ cup butter, softened
¾ cup sugar
1 egg
½ tablespoon grated lemon rind

1½ cups flour, sifted
¼ teaspoon salt
½ cup raspberry jam
1 egg yolk, beaten
powdered sugar, sifted

Cream butter and sugar together in a large bowl until light and fluffy. Beat in egg and lemon rind. Stir in flour and salt. Mix dough with hands until it holds together. Cover and refrigerate dough for 2 to 3 hours. Preheat oven to 375°F. On a lightly floured surface roll half of chilled dough to about ⅛-inch thickness. Cut out cookies with a floured 2-inch scalloped cookie cutter. Place cookie base on lightly greased baking sheet. Top each cookie with ½ teaspoon raspberry jam. Roll remaining half of dough and cut out cookies. Cut hole in center with 1-inch cutter to form rings. Place rings on top of jam-covered bottoms. Brush cookies lightly with beaten egg yolk. Bake in a preheated 375°F. oven for 8 to 10 minutes, or until lightly browned. Cool completely on wire rack. Dust with powdered sugar.

Yield: approximately 3 dozen.

Raspberry Flan

 Because a flan is really a custard pie, it needs to be eaten almost immediately. If there is any left over, it must be refrigerated.

1 cup milk
1/3 cup sugar
3 eggs
2 teaspoons vanilla
  pinch of salt

1/2 cup flour
3 cups raspberries,
  washed
powdered sugar

Preheat oven to 350°F.

Combine milk, 1/4 cup sugar, eggs, vanilla, salt, and flour in a blender and mix thoroughly, at high speed, for 1 minute. Pour a thin layer of batter into a lightly buttered, flameproof flan dish or deep pie plate. Cook over moderate heat until it sets. Remove dish from heat and spread with the raspberries. Sprinkle remaining sugar over berries. Pour remaining batter over the fruit and bake in a preheated 350°F oven for 50 to 60 minutes, or until browned. Sprinkle with powdered sugar and serve warm.

Yield: 6 servings.

Raspberry-Almond Coffee Ring

  This is my version of a recipe I have used for so many years—I can't even remember where the original came from. It is a moist, rich cake that is as good on the third day as on the first!

BATTER
¼ cup butter, softened
1 cup sugar
2 eggs, lightly beaten
1 teaspoon almond extract
2 cups flour

2 teaspoons baking powder
¼ teaspoon salt
1 teaspoon baking soda
1 cup sour cream

Preheat oven to 375°F.

Cream together ¼ cup butter and 1 cup sugar in a large bowl. Stir in 2 lightly beaten eggs. Stir in almond extract. Sift together flour, baking powder, and salt and blend into butter mixture. Stir baking soda into sour cream and allow to bubble for 1 minute. Stir sour cream into batter and blend thoroughly.

FILLING

2 cups raspberries

²/₃ cup sugar

1½ tablespoons
   cornstarch

2 tablespoons water

Crush raspberries in a small saucepan and add ²/₃ cup sugar. Dilute cornstarch in water and add to raspberries. Cook the fruit mixture over moderately high heat, stirring, until it is thick and clear. Cool. Spoon half of batter into greased tube pan. Spoon cooled raspberry mixture evenly over batter. Pour remaining batter on top.

TOPPING

½ cup sugar

¼ cup butter,
   softened

1 egg white

¼ cup honey

½ cup almonds, finely
   chopped

In a small bowl cream together ½ cup sugar and ¼ cup butter. Blend in egg white, honey, and finely chopped almonds. Spread topping on coffee ring and bake in a preheated 375°F. oven for 25 to 30 minutes.

Yield: 10 to 12 servings.

Raspberry Parfait

Don't wait until raspberry season to serve this because frozen fruit—if properly drained—can be substituted. Serve it in long-stemmed glasses so everyone can see the garnish of fruit at the bottom.

3 cups fresh
raspberries, washed
½ cup sugar
½ cup water

1 tablespoon grated
lemon peel
2 tablespoons kirsch
2 cups heavy cream,
whipped

Combine 2 cups raspberries, sugar, water, and lemon peel in a medium saucepan. Bring mixture to a boil, stirring, over moderate heat. Reduce heat and simmer for 5 minutes. Remove from heat and allow to cool. Press the mixture through a fine sieve. Stir kirsch into berry purée. Fold purée into whipped cream and beat until stiff. Divide 1 cup fresh raspberries among 8 stemmed glasses and spoon parfait over the fruit. Chill for 4 hours before serving.

Yield: 8 servings.

Raspberry Chantilly Squares

 A simple, frothy dessert to be made at least seven or eight hours ahead of the party. The original recipe came to me from a friend in Alaska—where the berries grow unusually large!

½ cup butter, melted
¼ cup brown sugar
1 cup flour
½ cup pecans, chopped
2 cups raspberries
2 egg whites

1 tablespoon lemon juice
¾ cup powdered sugar
1 teaspoon vanilla
1 cup heavy cream, whipped

Preheat oven to 350°F.

Mix together the butter, brown sugar, flour, and chopped nuts. Spread the mixture evenly in an 11-by-8-by-1-inch baking dish. Bake in a preheated 350°F. oven, stirring occasionally, for 20 minutes, or until golden brown. Remove half of nut mixture and reserve for topping. Spread remaining nut mixture evenly in the pan. In a large bowl combine raspberries, egg whites, lemon juice, powdered sugar, and vanilla. Beat with electric mixer for 10 to 15 minutes, or until mixture holds stiff peaks. Fold in whipped cream. Spoon cream mixture over nut mixture and smooth with a knife. Top with remaining nut mixture. Freeze for 6 to 8 hours before cutting into squares and serving.

Yield: 8 to 10 servings.

Classic Blackcap Pie

 Serve this pie warm so you can enjoy its full flavor. A small dollop of vanilla ice cream on top makes it even better.

4 cups wild black raspberries, washed	pastry for 9-inch, 2-crust pie
1¼ cups sugar	2 tablespoons butter
⅓ cup flour	

Preheat oven to 425°F.

Combine the berries with 1 cup sugar in a medium bowl and allow to stand for 30 minutes. Line a 9-inch pie plate with pastry. Combine flour with ¼ cup sugar and gently stir into berry mixture. Spoon berries into pastry-lined pie plate. Dot with butter. Cover with top crust, cut vents, and seal and flute edges to form high rim. Bake in a preheated 425°F. oven for 35 minutes, or until crust is golden.

Yield: 6 to 8 servings.

Raspberry-Pecan Bread

 Fruit breads—a plus at any meal—are also a nice addition to your picnic basket. Make this ahead and store in the freezer for the weekend.

½ cup butter
⅔ cup sugar
2 eggs
2 cups flour
1 teaspoon baking powder
½ teaspoon baking soda

½ teaspoon salt
¼ cup sour cream
1½ cups fresh raspberries, washed
½ cup pecans, chopped

Preheat oven to 350°F.

Cream together the butter and sugar in a large bowl. Add eggs and beat the mixture until light and fluffy. Sift together flour, baking powder, baking soda, and salt. Stir flour mixture into egg mixture, alternately with sour cream. Fold raspberries and pecans into batter. Pour batter into a greased 9-by-5-by-3-inch loaf pan. Bake the bread in a preheated 350°F. oven for 45 to 50 minutes, or until it is golden. Allow bread to cool in pan for 10 minutes before turning on rack. Cool completely before slicing.

Yield: 1 loaf.

Linzer Torte

This rich Viennese dessert that looks like a jam pie was named for the Austrian city of Linz. You don't have to travel to the Danube, however, to enjoy the aroma and taste of this classic pastry.

1 cup butter, softened
1 cup sugar
2 egg yolks, beaten
1 cup unblanched almonds, finely ground
2 teaspoons grated orange rind
2 teaspoons grated lemon rind

1½ cups flour, sifted
3 teaspoons cinnamon
½ teaspoon ground cloves
1 cup raspberry jam powdered sugar, sifted

Cream together the softened butter and 1 cup sugar in a large bowl. Stir in egg yolks, ground almonds, and orange and lemon rinds. Beat until mixture is light and fluffy. Sift together flour and spices and gradually beat into the creamed mixture. Continue beating until mixture is smooth. Cover with plastic wrap and refrigerate dough for 2 hours, or until firm. Remove ²/₃rds of the dough from refrigerator and press it to ½-inch thickness over the bottom and sides of a 9-inch springform pan. Spoon in jam and spread evenly over shell. Roll remaining dough on a floured surface. Cut lattice strips and secure them over filling. Bake in a preheated 350°F oven for 45 to 50 minutes. Cool. Remove sides of pan and dust with powdered sugar. Cut the torte into thin wedges and serve.

Yield: 12 to 15 servings.

Raspberry-Cherry Conserve

 A jar of this bright red conserve—tied with a green ribbon—makes a pretty and appetizing gift for someone you like.

4 cups raspberries, washed

3 cups sweet cherries, pitted

3 cups sugar

¼ cup lemon juice

¼ teaspoon almond extract

½ cup almonds, blanched and slivered

Press the raspberries through a sieve to remove seeds. Lightly crush the cherries in a large Dutch oven and simmer them in their own juice until tender. Add raspberry pulp, sugar, and lemon juice. Simmer gently, uncovered, stirring occasionally, until mixture is thick for about 1 hour. Stir in almond extract and almonds and simmer, stirring, for 2 minutes. Remove from heat. Ladle hot conserve into hot, sterilized jars. Adjust lids and process in boiling water bath for 5 minutes.

Yield: 6 half-pints.

Raspberry Sauce

 For an extraordinary dessert serve this sauce over ice-cream-filled meringues.

2 cups fresh
raspberries, washed

1 cup sugar

2 tablespoons
cornstarch

2 tablespoons cold
water

1 teaspoon lemon
juice

Combine raspberries with sugar in a medium saucepan and heat, stirring frequently, to a boil. Mix cornstarch with water and stir into berries. Cook, stirring, until thickened. Remove from heat and stir in lemon juice. Refrigerate before serving.

Yield: 2 cups.

Audrey's Raspberry Surprise

 This recipe is based on one that was given to me by an elegant Omaha woman who serves it as a dessert. So not to miss any fun at your own party, combine the ingredients hours in advance and store in the freezer. Blend the "surprise" just before serving.

¼ cup coffee-flavored
liqueur

2 scoops vanilla ice
cream

½ cup club soda

½ cup fresh
raspberries, washed

Combine all the ingredients in a blender. Blend thoroughly until the mixture is frothy. Serve in champagne glasses as a liquid dessert.

Yield: 2 servings.

Blackcap Jam

Of the berry jams, this is the family favorite! For a welcome gift package, arrange a pretty jar of jam with packages of unusual tea and English biscuits in a tea caddy.

2 quarts wild black
   raspberries, washed
   and picked over
2 tablespoons lemon
   juice

6 cups sugar
½ bottle liquid fruit
   pectin

Crush the berries and measure 4 cups of pulp into a large Dutch oven. Stir in lemon juice. Add sugar, mixing well. Bring mixture to a full rolling boil over high heat. Boil hard for 1 minute, stirring constantly. Remove from heat. Immediately stir in liquid pectin. Alternately stir and skim off foam for 5 minutes. Ladle the hot mixture into hot, sterilized jars, leaving a ½-inch head space. Cover with melted paraffin.

Yield: 7 half-pints.

Apricot-Blackcap Marmalade

I first tried this when I had a bumper harvest of blackcaps and a friend arrived with a basket of homegrown apricots that needed to be put up quickly. The result was a very thick marmalade that becomes a whole meal when it tops thick slices of fresh-from-the-oven bread.

4 cups pitted and diced fresh apricots

2 cups wild black raspberries, washed

¼ cup orange juice

7 cups granulated sugar

1 bottle liquid fruit pectin

Combine the prepared apricots, raspberries, and orange juice in a large Dutch oven. Mix thoroughly and place over high heat. Bring to a full, rolling boil, stirring constantly, and boil hard for 1 minute. Remove from heat and immediately stir in fruit pectin. Stir and skim off foam for 5 to 10 minutes to cool slightly and prevent floating fruit. Quickly ladle into hot, sterilized jars and seal at once with ¼-inch melted paraffin.

Yield: 8 to 9 half-pints.

Raspberry Shrub

This was the classic summer refresher that was so popular during Grandmother's time. In the days before refrigeration, bottles of this pink concentrate were stored in the root cellar—under the kitchen—ready for afternoon guests on the veranda.

3 pints fresh raspberries, washed	3 cups cider vinegar sugar

Place the raspberries in a stone crock or large jar. Pour vinegar over the fruit and allow to stand overnight. The next day strain and measure the juice. To each pint of juice add 2 cups sugar. Boil 10 minutes. Pour the hot concentrate into sterilized jars and seal. When serving, fill a beverage glass $1/3$ full of concentrate and dilute with ice water.

Yield: approximately 3 pints.

Raspberry Punch

A crowd pleaser for summer barbecues, this punch can be made with frozen raspberries. Combine the juices a day early and store in a gallon jug in the refrigerator. As the guests arrive, pour the fruit base into a punch bowl and add ginger ale.

2 pints fresh
 raspberries,
 crushed, or 4 cups
 frozen raspberries
1 cup water
3 cups orange juice

3 cups pineapple juice
1 quart ginger ale,
 chilled
whole raspberries

Combine crushed raspberries with water in a medium saucepan. Bring to a boil and remove from heat. Cool. Work berries through a fine sieve. Combine raspberry purée with orange and pineapple juices, stirring to blend. Chill. Just before serving, add ginger ale. Serve in punch bowl garnished with fresh whole raspberries.

Yield: approximately 20 to 25 servings.

Raspberry Rosé

This is a light, fruity wine that serves as a fine table wine as well as being a good addition to the punch bowl.

5 cups raspberries, washed
1 gallon boiling water
1 Campden tablet, crushed
1 teaspoon pectic enzyme

5 cups sugar
½ teaspoon yeast nutrient
1 package dry wine yeast

Crush the raspberries in a crock and add boiling water. Stir and set aside to cool. When mixture has cooled to room temperature, add the crushed Campden tablet and pectic enzyme. Cover with plastic wrap and store in a dark place for 4 days, pressing down the floating fruit daily. On the fifth day strain the mixture through a jelly bag into a clean crock, squeezing to extract all juice. Add sugar to the strained liquid, stirring to dissolve. Add yeast nutrient and yeast. Transfer mixture to a clear gallon jug and, leaving a 3-inch head space, secure fermentation lock in place. Store in a dark place at room temperature for 2 to 3 weeks, or until violent fermentation ceases. Siphon into a clean gallon jug and store for 3 months. Repeat racking process twice more at 3-month intervals. Bottle wine at the end of the ninth month.

Yield: 1 gallon.

Raspberry Fizz

This is a delicious variation of the Ramos Gin Fizz that originated in New Orleans at the turn of the century; it is a good beginning for a relaxed luncheon.

½ cup raspberries, washed

1½ ounces gin

juice of ½ orange

1 teaspoon powdered sugar

soda water

fresh mint

Crush raspberries and work through a fine sieve into a cocktail shaker. Add gin, orange juice, and sugar. Cover the container and shake well. Pour into a glass with crushed ice. Fill glass with chilled soda water and garnish with fresh mint.

Yield: 1 serving.

Chapter Eight
The Divine Berry

Of strawberries, it has been said that "God could doubtless have made a better berry but doubtless he never did." Whether this enthusiastic tribute to the heart-shaped berry was first uttered by Jonathan Swift or William Butler, there is little disagreement with the sentiment. The red, fleshy fruit with the external seeds is popular not only for its aroma and flavor but for its general association with warm summer days.

The arrival of summer for our family is officially celebrated on "strawberry night," a custom that is as eagerly anticipated by the adults as the children. On that special day in June, after picking and filling the refrigerator with quarts of berries, we sit down to an "as-much-as-you-like" supper of Old-Fashioned Strawberry Shortcake (page 187). Our evening of indulgence, I suspect, will be remembered by our children longer than any gourmet feast I might prepare.

The early Christians, however, would not have allowed themselves such delicious excess. It was commonly believed by them that the Virgin Mary had a special fondness for strawberries and would cast into eternal torment any mother who arrived at heaven's gate with the berry stain on her lips. The superstition was further embellished with the belief that when an infant died, he ascended to heaven disguised as a strawberry. Rather than commit cannibalism, it was safer to avoid eating the fruit. This close association between strawberries and divinity may have been the reason so many of the English nobility chose to decorate their coronets and coats-of-arms with the design of the strawberry plant!

The small, wild strawberry, which grows abundantly throughout Europe, was noticed as early as the fourteenth century when Charles V ordered twelve thousand plants to be set in the French royal gardens. Although the flavor of the delicate fruit was probably appreciated as much then as it is today, some of the interest in strawberries was due to the medicinal properties that were attributed to the plant. Gastritis, aching joints, and loose teeth were only some of the ailments thought to be relieved by strawberry brews.

Strawberries are very high in vitamin C but the level is greatly decreased when the fruit is damaged or allowed to stand, unused, for several days. Cooking the berries, as in jams, causes the loss of most of the natural vitamins. Interestingly, this same fruit, which has been regarded as a healing agent and is high in vitamins, is the one fruit that commonly induces hives in so many people.

The large, cultivated berry that we know today was developed in the United States from a South American species. During the late eighteenth century, a naval officer, returning to his native France, carried with him some of the plants he had seen in Chile. From those ancestors were bred the commercial fruit that can withstand the shipping and storage of today's market.

Strawberry designs, used to decorate clothing, bed sheets, and paper napkins, have made this plant recognizable to most people. The mother plant is really a perennial herb that sends out runners, or creeping stems, that take root and form new plants. Each stem, bearing three serrated leaflets, comes directly off the root, forming a crown, or mother plant. The small white blossoms yield to red berries in June or July.

Strawberry plants need a minimum of six hours of sunshine daily and well-drained soil. It is interesting to note that the quantity of vitamin C in the fruit increases in direct proportion to the amount of sunlight the plant receives during the last few days before harvest.

June-bearers, as the name implies, yield one heavy harvest in June. The first year the plants are in the ground, the blossoms should be plucked and not allowed to bear fruit. This variety of strawberry quickly produces new plants that eventually increase the annual harvest.

Everbearers have the advantage of a longer harvesting season, producing a crop in June, a scattering of berries throughout the summer, and another large crop in early fall.

Whatever variety the home gardener selects, it is necessary to cover the surrounding soil of the established plants with straw. Colder climates require a heavy mulching for the winter months. As the weather warms and the plants turn green in the spring, the mulch should be loosened, but not removed. It may be the traditional practice of mulching with straw that was responsible for the name "strawberry!"

Because the plants are so adaptable, city dwellers can enjoy growing strawberries in a very limited space. If the basic requirements of sun and drainage are satisfied, the plants will thrive in hanging pots or wooden barrels. The plants, in addition to providing fruit for breakfast, will add a decorative, country charm to any apartment terrace.

Glazed Strawberries

 Don't try this on a rainy or hot, humid day—the glaze may not harden. The berries should be perfect— with no surface nicks—and must be dry to hold the glaze.

2 cups sugar
⅔ cup water
⅛ teaspoon cream of
tartar

1 quart large, perfect
strawberries with
stems, washed and
patted dry

Combine sugar and water in top of double boiler. Stirring, heat to a boil over moderate heat, until sugar dissolves. Mix cream of tartar with 1 teaspoon water and stir into boiling syrup. When syrup reaches 290°F. on candy thermometer, place pan over hot water. Holding berries by stems, dip fruit into syrup. Turn berry to completely coat, allowing any excess to drip into pan. Rest berries on stem-end, on oiled wax paper, to dry. Serve within 2 to 4 hours.

Yield: 6 servings.

Strawberry Fritters

Although this requires last minute preparation, it is worth the effort when you hear your guests' appreciative compliments. The batter can be made early in the day and refrigerated until cooking time.

1 quart fresh
  strawberries
1 egg, lightly beaten
1¼ cups milk

½ cup cooking oil
1 cup flour, sifted
  powdered sugar
  oil (for frying)

Wash strawberries and pat dry with paper towels. Remove stems. Combine egg, milk, cooking oil, and flour in a bowl and mix until batter is smooth. Dip whole berries in batter and fry in hot oil (375°F.) for 2 to 3 minutes, or until coating is golden and crisp. Drain the fried berries on paper towels and dust with powdered sugar. Serve hot.

Yield: 6 servings.

Strawberry Buffet Dips

 This is an impressive addition to any party but is especially appropriate for a bridal shower. Use your prettiest serving dishes to make it the centerpiece of a buffet table.

3 quarts large, perfect
  strawberries
fresh mint

Wash and dry the strawberries, leaving the stems on. Arrange the berries in 2 large brandy snifters or on a large platter. Garnish the berries with sprigs of fresh mint and surround with bowls of dip.

Sour Cream Dip

1 cup sour cream
2 tablespoons
  powdered sugar

orange-flavored liqueur
  thin slices of
  orange peel

Thoroughly combine the sour cream, sugar, and liqueur. Spoon into a small bowl and garnish with thin twists of orange peel.

Whipped Cream Dip

1 cup heavy cream
1 tablespoon
  powdered sugar

½ teaspoon vanilla
  extract
cinnamon

Whip together heavy cream, powdered sugar, and vanilla extract. Spoon into a small bowl and sprinkle with cinnamon.

Almond Cheese Dip

1 8-ounce package
  cream cheese,
  softened
  sour cream
  almond-flavored
  liqueur

3 tablespoons
  almonds, finely
  chopped
  almonds, slivered

Dilute the cream cheese to dipping consistency with sour cream. Blend in liqueur to taste. Stir in chopped almonds and garnish with a few slivered almonds.

Yield: 8 to 10 servings.

Strawberry Tea Sandwiches

 These delicate treats are a carry-over from my childhood. We serve them as an appetizer with a tray of soft, mild cheese.

1 cup strawberries, washed and hulled

fine sugar

20 slices sponge cake, 1½ by 3 inches, trimmed

½ cup heavy cream, whipped

Slice the strawberries and sprinkle with fine sugar. Spread half the cake slices thinly with whipped cream. Cover cream with a layer of strawberry slices. Arrange the remaining cake slices on top of the strawberries and lightly press them together. Serve immediately.

Yield: 10 tea sandwiches.

Sour Cream Strawberry Soup

 A delicately flavored and colored soup, this is perfect for a prewedding luncheon. Its adaptability allows you to serve it as a prelude to the entrée or as a dessert.

4 cups strawberries, washed and hulled	1 tablespoon cornstarch
3 cups plus 2 tablespoons water	1 cup sour cream
½ cup sugar	sliced strawberries
1 cup orange juice	grated orange rind

Combine 4 cups strawberries, 3 cups water, and sugar in a large saucepan. Bring the mixture to a boil, reduce heat, and simmer for 5 minutes. Stir in orange juice. Add cornstarch mixed with 2 tablespoons water and simmer, stirring for 10 minutes, or until soup is slightly thickened. Refrigerate. Pour the chilled soup into a blender and mix at high speed until the liquid is smooth. Stir in sour cream. Chill for 3 to 4 hours. Garnish each serving with sliced strawberries and freshly grated orange rind.

Yield: 6 to 8 servings.

Blender Bisque

 Here is your chance to have "summer in a bowl!"
Serve this with a cheese soufflé and spinach salad for a
patio luncheon.

3 cups strawberries,
washed and hulled

1½ cups water

¾ cup sugar

3 tablespoons lemon
juice

1 teaspoon grated
lemon peel

1½ cups red wine

1 cup yogurt

fresh mint

Combine strawberries, ½ cup water, and sugar in a
blender. Cover and blend the mixture until it is puréed.
Stir in lemon juice, lemon peel, 1 cup water, and red
wine. Stir in yogurt until blended. Chill the soup for
several hours before serving and garnish with fresh
mint.

Yield: 6 servings.

Strawberry Salad Mold

 This "make-ahead" salad can be prepared any time of the year by substituting frozen berries for the fresh fruit. Light and sweet, it could be mistaken for dessert by berry lovers!

2 egg yolks
2 teaspoons
   granulated sugar
2 tablespoons lemon
   juice
6 marshmallows
1 cup heavy cream,
   whipped

2 cups strawberries,
   hulled, washed, and
   well drained
¾ cup walnuts,
   chopped
whole strawberries
   for garnish

In the top of a double boiler combine egg yolks, sugar, and lemon juice. Cook, stirring, over moderate heat for 10 minutes, or until mixture coats the spoon. Add marshmallows and beat with a whisk until smooth. Cool. Fold the whipped cream into the marshmallow mixture. Slice the berries. Fold the sliced berries and chopped nuts into the marshmallow mixture and pour into a 1-quart mold. Refrigerate overnight. Garnish with whole, perfect berries when ready to serve.

Yield: 6 servings.

Fresh Strawberry Salad

This salad always reminds me of California—perhaps because it is so easy to prepare and refreshing to eat!

1 quart strawberries, washed, hulled, and sliced

1 fresh pineapple, peeled, cored, and cut in chunks

2 bananas, peeled and sliced

1 cup coconut, shredded

½ cup walnuts, chopped

½ cup powdered sugar

½ cup orange juice, chilled

1 cup yogurt, chilled

Combine berries, pineapple chunks, banana slices, coconut, and walnuts in a bowl. Sprinkle sugar over fruit and toss well. Mix together orange juice and yogurt and pour over fruit mixture. Toss to mix.

Yield: 8 servings.

Berry Best Salad in Orange Cups

 A salad for dedicated berry fanciers! For a festive party look, cut the edges of the orange cups in a sawtooth fashion.

1½ cups yogurt
¼ cup honey
1 tablespoon grated orange peel
3 tablespoons orange juice
½ teaspoon grated nutmeg
6 large oranges

1 cup fresh blueberries, washed and picked over
1 cup fresh raspberries, washed
2 cups fresh strawberries, washed and hulled
fresh mint

Thoroughly blend together yogurt, honey, orange peel and juice, and nutmeg. Refrigerate for several hours. Cut oranges in half and remove the pulp. Trim the bottom of each orange half so it will stand. Combine berries with as much orange pulp as desired and spoon into orange shells. Spoon dressing over berries when ready to serve. Garnish each salad with a sprig of fresh mint.

Yield: 12 servings.

Almond Crepes with Strawberries

Crepes are so easy to prepare, I don't know why we wait for special occasions to serve them. This is an elegant luncheon entrée or dessert.

1 cup flour, sifted	2 eggs, lightly beaten
½ teaspoon salt	1¼ cups milk
1 teaspoon baking powder	½ cup toasted almonds, finely chopped
2 tablespoons powdered sugar	butter, melted

Combine flour, salt, baking powder, and powdered sugar and sift into a mixing bowl. Combine eggs and milk and stir into dry ingredients. Mix just until dry ingredients are moistened. Stir in chopped almonds. Cook the crepes, one at a time, in a buttered 5-inch crepe pan or round-bottomed skillet.

Strawberry-Sour Cream Filling

2 cups sour cream	3 cups strawberries, sliced and sweetened
3 tablespoons powdered sugar	butter
2 tablespoons almond-flavored liqueur	powdered sugar for dusting

Combine sour cream, powdered sugar, and liqueur. Spread crepes with sour cream mixture and a generous portion of strawberries. Roll crepes closed and arrange in a buttered chafing dish over direct heat. Add remaining strawberries and heat crepes, turning carefully. Dust with powdered sugar before serving.

Yield: 16 crepes.

Tropical Ham

  You don't have to live in the tropics to appreciate the sweet and sour flavor of this quick-to-fix supper. This can also be prepared in heavy foil and cooked on the outdoor grill, and would be delicious served with rice pilaf and buttered peas with onions.

1 ham steak (1½–2 inches thick)

1 cup fresh peach slices

½ cup Spiced Fruit Conserve (page 194)

¼ cup coconut, shredded

⅓ cup sherry

1½ tablespoons wine vinegar

Preheat oven to 375°F.

Place the ham in a shallow baking dish. Top with peach slices. Spread Spiced Fruit Conserve over peaches and sprinkle with coconut. Pour sherry and vinegar over all. Bake in a preheated 375°F. oven for 20 to 25 minutes.

Yield: 2 to 3 servings.

Rich Strawberry Bars

This is the richest, melt-in-your-mouth pastry cookie you can make. Store them in the refrigerator—if they are not gone before they are cool!

1 cup butter, softened	2 tablespoons cornstarch
2 cups flour	
½ cup sour cream	3 cups strawberries, washed, hulled, and sliced
½ teaspoon vanilla extract	
⅔ cup sugar	powdered sugar

Cut butter into flour with a pastry blender. Add sour cream and vanilla extract, mixing well. Dough will be stiff. Cover dough and refrigerate for 2 hours. Combine sugar and cornstarch in a medium saucepan. Stir in sliced strawberries. Stirring constantly, cook over low heat until mixture is thickened and clear. Cool. Divide the chilled dough in half and roll one portion into a 12-by-8-inch rectangle on a floured board. Line a 12-by-8-by-2-inch pan with the dough and spread evenly with the strawberry mixture. Roll remaining dough to fit and place over filling. Bake in a preheated 325°F. oven for 50 minutes, or until golden brown. Cool. Dust with powdered sugar and cut into bars.

Yield: 2½ dozen.

Old-Fashioned Strawberry Shortcake

This recipe is the center of attention on our annual "strawberry night." My children claim that the only thing better is Christmas!

2 cups flour
4 teaspoons baking
　powder
½ teaspoon salt
1 tablespoon sugar
⅓ cup shortening,
　softened
1 egg, well beaten

⅔ cup milk
　sugar
3 pints strawberries,
　washed, hulled, and
　sliced
heavy or whipped
　cream

Preheat oven to 425°F.

Sift together flour, baking powder, salt, and 1 tablespoon sugar into a medium bowl. Cut in shortening. Combine egg and milk and stir into flour mixture, until just blended. Turn dough out on floured surface and knead lightly for 1 minute. Pat dough to ½-inch thickness and cut with biscuit cutter. Arrange first layer in a greased 9-inch pan. Top each biscuit with another, and bake in a preheated 425°F. oven for 20 minutes. Allow to cool slightly. Sugar the berry slices to taste and allow to stand for 10 minutes. When ready to serve, split the biscuits and spoon berries between and over each biscuit. Top with heavy cream or whipped cream.

Yield: 6 servings.

Cheesecake Melba

This is a favorite cheesecake in our house. Although it is unorthodox, I have been known to eat the single leftover piece for breakfast!

1½ cups graham cracker crumbs

¼ cup butter, melted

1½ cups plus 2 tablespoons sugar

½ teaspoon cinnamon

2 8-ounce packages cream cheese, softened

3 eggs

1 cup sour cream

½ teaspoon vanilla

1 cup raspberries, crushed

1½ tablespoons cornstarch

2 tablespoons lemon juice, strained

2 cups perfect strawberries, washed and hulled

Preheat oven to 350°F.

Combine cracker crumbs, melted butter, ¼ cup sugar, and cinnamon in a small bowl. Press mixture over bottom and sides of a buttered, deep 9-inch pie plate. In a large bowl beat cream cheese with electric mixer until soft. Beat in eggs, one at a time. Gradually beat in ½ cup sugar and continue beating until smooth. Pour cheese mixture into pie shell. Bake in a preheated 350°F. oven for 20 minutes. Remove from oven and cool on wire rack for 15 minutes. Combine sour cream, 2 tablespoons sugar, and vanilla in a small bowl. Spread over baked cheesecake. Bake in oven at 475°F. for 5 minutes. Cool on rack 30 minutes. Work the crushed raspberries through a fine sieve into a saucepan. Stir in ¾ cup sugar. Dissolve cornstarch in lemon juice and add to purée. Cook over moderate heat, stirring, until mixture is thickened. Arrange strawberries on cheesecake and spoon cooled raspberry mixture over the top. Chill for several hours before serving.

Yield: 6 to 8 servings.

Winter Strawberries

Because these are colorful and tasty, they are a fine addition to an assortment of Christmas cookies, or pile them in an old-fashioned berry basket for an edible centerpiece. They look like the real thing!

1 15-ounce can sweetened condensed milk	1 cup walnuts, finely chopped
	red colored sugar
3 3-ounce packages strawberry-flavored gelatin	3 drops green food coloring
1½ cups coconut, shredded	1 tablespoon water
	¾ cup almonds, slivered

Blend together the milk, gelatin, coconut, and chopped walnuts. Wrap dough securely in plastic wrap and chill in refrigerator for 24 hours. Remove from refrigerator and shape dough into the shape of strawberries, using approximately 1½ teaspoons dough for each "berry." Roll "strawberries" in red sugar to coat. Combine green food coloring with water and soak almonds in the mixture until green. Arrange green almonds in place as strawberry stems.

Yield: 3 dozen.

Fresh Strawberry Pie

Shimmering red, this is my personal favorite of the berry pies. Even the early Christians couldn't have resisted such temptation!

½ cup butter, melted
1¼ cups sugar
1½ cups graham cracker crumbs
1 teaspoon cinnamon

2 quarts strawberries, washed and hulled
3 tablespoons cornstarch
1 cup heavy cream, whipped

Combine the melted butter and ¼ cup sugar in a medium bowl. Add cracker crumbs and cinnamon and mix well. Press over bottom and side of buttered 9-inch pie plate. In a saucepan mash 1 quart of berries. Add 1 cup sugar and cornstarch. Cook over moderate heat, stirring, until the mixture is clear and thickened. Fill lined pie plate with remaining quart of strawberries. Pour cooked berry mixture over and chill for several hours before serving with whipped cream.

Yield: 6 servings.

Strawberry Trifle

A classic English favorite. Sinfully rich, but worth every calorie!

2 teaspoons grated lemon peel
⅓ cup fresh lemon juice
½ cup sugar
½ cup butter
3 eggs, lightly beaten

1 cup sour cream
ladyfingers
2 cups strawberries, washed, hulled, and sliced
¼ toasted almonds, slivered
fresh strawberries

Combine lemon peel, lemon juice, sugar, and butter in a saucepan and cook over low heat, stirring occasionally, until butter is melted and sugar dissolved. Remove from heat. Slowly stir beaten eggs into lemon mixture and cook over medium heat, stirring constantly, until mixture thickens slightly. Do not boil. Remove from heat. When cool, stir in sour cream. Split ladyfingers and stand up around sides of 8-inch springform pan. Line bottom of pan with ladyfingers. Layer half of sliced strawberries over ladyfingers and cover with 1 cup cooled lemon sauce. Sprinkle with half the almonds. Repeat the layers, ending with lemon sauce. Garnish with whole strawberries and remainder of almonds. Chill for several hours before serving.

Yield: 8 to 10 servings.

Fresh Strawberry Ice Cream

What better way to spend a warm June evening than making your own Strawberry Ice Cream! For variety, add ¼ cup orange-flavored liqueur or the crunch of chopped pistachio nuts.

2 quarts strawberries,
  washed and hulled
1¼ cups sugar
  juice of ½ lemon
2 cups light cream
2 cups heavy cream

Slice the strawberries. Force the fruit through a fine sieve into a large bowl. Add sugar and lemon juice. Thoroughly stir in light and heavy creams. Cover and refrigerate for several hours, or overnight. When ready to churn, ladle the chilled cream mixture into the container of a crank freezer and crank until the mixture is thick. Pack ice cream in plastic containers and store in freezer.

Yield: 1 gallon.

Strawberries Romanoff

An effortless, delicious dessert—it is easy to understand why it has become a classic.

1 quart fresh strawberries, washed and hulled

¹/₃ cup powdered sugar

6 tablespoons orange-flavored liqueur

1 cup orange juice, freshly squeezed

1 cup heavy cream, whipped

whole strawberries, with stems, for garnish

Drain the strawberries and place in a medium bowl. Sprinkle sugar over fruit and add liqueur and orange juice. Toss gently, and allow to stand for 1 hour, stirring occasionally. When ready to serve, drain some of the liquid off berries. Spoon berries into chilled serving dish and fold in whipped cream. Garnish with whole, perfect strawberries. Serve immediately.

Yield: 6 servings.

Spiced Fruit Conserve

This is good with any cold meat or use it as a glaze for ham.

2 cups pineapple, finely chopped

2 oranges, seeded and finely chopped

4 cups sugar

¼ teaspoon cinnamon

¼ teaspoon allspice

⅛ teaspoon ground cloves

1 quart strawberries, washed and hulled

¾ cup almonds, slivered

Combine chopped pineapple, oranges, sugar, and spices in a large Dutch oven over low heat. Bring mixture to a boil slowly, stirring, until sugar is dissolved. Gently boil the mixture for 15 minutes. Stir in berries and continue cooking for 20 to 25 minutes, or until mixture thickens. Stir frequently to prevent scorching. Stir in almonds during last few minutes of cooking. Ladle hot conserve into hot, sterilized jars and cover with melted paraffin.

Yield: 6 half-pints.

Strawberry Jelly

   The ruby red color of this jelly makes it an attractive Christmas offering. Make enough for yourself so you can have pampered breakfasts of warm croissants and strawberry jelly throughout the winter.

2½ quarts very ripe
   strawberries,
   washed and hulled
7½ cups sugar

¼ cup lemon juice,
   strained
1 bottle liquid fruit
   pectin

Crush the berries in a large bowl. Place the crushed fruit in a jelly bag and squeeze out juice. Measure 4 cups juice into a large Dutch oven. Stir in sugar and lemon juice. Bring mixture to a boil over high heat, stirring constantly. Immediately stir in liquid pectin. Bring mixture to a full, rolling boil and boil hard for 1 minute, stirring constantly. Remove from heat. Stir and skim off foam with a metal spoon. Pour hot jelly into hot, sterilized jars, leaving a ½-inch head space. Cover immediately with melted paraffin.

Yield: 8 half-pints.

Strawberry-Peach Jam

When the fruits are in season, I make a lot of this for Christmas giving. The peaches look like bits of gold floating among the berries!

2½ pints strawberries, washed and hulled

½ pound fully ripe peaches, skinned and pitted

¼ cup lemon juice

7½ cups sugar

1 bottle liquid fruit pectin

Crush the strawberries and measure 3 cups into a large Dutch oven. Finely chop the peaches. Measure 1 cup chopped peaches and add to strawberries. Stir lemon juice into fruit mixture. Thoroughly stir sugar into fruit and place over high heat. Bring to a full rolling boil and boil hard for 1 minute, stirring constantly. Remove from heat and immediately stir in fruit pectin. Stir and skim off foam for 5 to 10 minutes. Ladle jam into hot, sterilized jars, leaving a ½-inch head space. Seal with melted paraffin.

Yield: 8 half-pints.

Strawberry-Rhubarb Sauce

 When afternoon tea was a tradition in Grandmother's house, this sauce was spooned onto hot biscuits. We like it for pancakes and waffles.

1½ pounds rhubarb, washed and cut into 1-inch pieces

1 quart strawberries, washed, hulled, and halved

1¼ cups sugar

¼ cup water

2½ teaspoons lemon juice

Combine all the ingredients in a 6-quart Dutch oven and bring to a boil over medium heat. Boil for 1 minute. Ladle the hot sauce into hot, sterilized jars, leaving a ½-inch head space. Adjust lids and process in boiling water bath for 15 minutes.

Yield: 6 to 7 half-pints.

Strawberry-Banana Cooler

 Strawberries and bananas are a favorite fruit combination for many people—especially my children. This thick, airy drink is like a milk shake but it is nutritious enough for breakfast.

2 cups fresh strawberries, hulled and sliced	2 tablespoons honey
	2 cups milk, chilled
2 bananas, peeled and mashed	1 cup yogurt, chilled
	grated nutmeg

Combine all the ingredients except nutmeg in a blender. Blend until thoroughly mixed and smooth. Serve in chilled glasses and garnish with grated nutmeg.

Yield: 6 servings.

Strawberry Breakfast Nog

 Although this began as a breakfast drink for an egg-hating daughter, I have found it a satisfying—and delicious—lunch substitute on busy days. The bonus is that it provides energy without a lot of calories.

1 cup fresh strawberries, washed and hulled	2 cups cold milk
	1 pineapple ring, halved
1 cup pineapple juice	2 whole strawberries
1 egg	

Combine strawberries, pineapple juice, egg, and milk in a blender. Thoroughly blend until smooth. Pour into chilled tall glasses and garnish each with half a pineapple ring and a whole strawberry.

Yield: 2 servings.

Strawberry Champagne Punch

 A delicate and festive blend, Strawberry Champagne Punch is traditionally associated with weddings and June parties. It is worth planning a celebration so you can serve this.

    2 quarts fresh
      strawberries, hulled
      and sliced
    1 cup fine sugar
    1 bottle white wine
      ice ring
    1 cup kirsch
    2 bottles champagne,
      chilled

Combine the sliced strawberries and sugar in a large bowl. Cover with white wine and allow to stand for several hours. Make an ice ring for the punch bowl by freezing water in a metal ring or tube pan. When ready to serve, invert the ice mold and wrap a hot wet towel around the pan until the ring slips out of the mold. Arrange ice ring in a punch bowl and add strawberries and wine. Stir in kirsch. Add chilled champagne.

Yield: approximately 25 servings.

Strawberry-Cherry Liqueur

Rich in berry color and taste, this liqueur is excellent in trifle or served over ice cream.

2 cups strawberries,
hulled and crushed

2 cups sweet cherries,
crushed, but not
pitted

1 3-inch stick
cinnamon

1¾ cups sugar

2 quarts rosé

2 cups vodka

Thoroughly combine all the ingredients in a wide-mouthed glass container with a tight-fitting lid. Allow mixture to stand at room temperature for 48 hours, inverting bottle occasionally. Strain mixture through a jelly bag into bottles, squeezing to extract all the liquid. Cork tightly and allow to mellow for 30 days before serving.

Yield: approximately 3 quarts.

Strawberry Dessert Wine

The aroma and taste of this wine leave no doubt that it was made from "divine berries." Because of its sweetness, it is best served as a sherry or dessert wine.

4 quarts ripe
  strawberries,
  washed and hulled
1 cup raisins,
  chopped
4 quarts boiling water

4 pounds sugar
  juice of 2 lemons
1 package dry wine
  yeast
1 Campden tablet,
  crushed

Crush strawberries in a large crock. Add raisins. Pour boiling water over fruit and allow to cool to room temperature. Squeezing to extract all juice, strain the cooled mixture through a jelly bag into a 3-gallon fermenting crock. Add sugar and stir until dissolved. Stir in lemon juice. Add wine yeast. Cover with plastic wrap, sealing tightly, and store in a dark place for 5 days, pressing down cap twice daily. On the sixth day siphon the wine into a clear gallon jug, taking care to avoid bottom sediment. Leaving a 3-inch head space, secure fermentation lock in place. Store in a dark place for 1 month, or until violent fermentation stops. Rack into a clean gallon jug. Fill to the top, add Campden tablet, and seal. Repeat racking process twice more at 3-month intervals. Bottle wine at the end of the ninth month. Wine may be served at any time after the ninth month, but it improves appreciably if allowed to age in the bottles for another year.

Yield: 6 bottles.

Chapter Nine
The Odd Berries

Although wild berries have been used through the years as a source of food, many are not recognized as edible because they are regional in distribution or grow in limited quantities. These are the odd berries. Few of us would be able to identify a patch of serviceberries, crowberries, or bearberries, yet they are good survival foods and can be cooked into jams and jellies for table use. Remember though, no berry should be eaten unless you are very sure of the variety.

ELDERBERRIES

These round purplish black berries, very similar in appearance to blueberries, were popular long before elderberry wine was made famous in *Arsenic and Old Lace.* The shrubs grow from five to twelve feet in height and produce star-shaped white flowers in June and July. The large clusters of berries quickly fill harvesting pails in September and late fall, providing fruit for pies, pancakes, jelly, and muffins.

Easily cultivated in the home garden, elderberry bushes need to be planted in sun or lightly shaded areas, three to four feet apart. If properly pruned, the bushes will provide a luxuriant, dense hedge, in addition to an abundant supply of fruit. By dipping the tender blossoms in batter and deep frying them, even the flowers can be used in your summer menu.

Elderberry Soup

A Scandinavian favorite!

3 cups ripe elderberries, washed and picked over

5 cups water plus 2 tablespoons cold water

¾ cup sugar

grated rind and juice of ½ lemon

1 2-inch stick cinnamon

1 tablespoon cornstarch

sour cream

cinnamon

Combine the berries in a saucepan with 5 cups water and bring to a boil over high heat. Reduce heat and simmer for 30 to 40 minutes, or until berries are soft and easily mashed. Work the berries through a fine sieve. Combine the elderberry purée and liquid, sugar, lemon rind and juice, and cinnamon stick in another saucepan. Dilute cornstarch in 2 tablespoons cold water and blend into the soup. Stirring, simmer the soup until thickened. Discard cinnamon stick. Serve soup warm with sour cream and sprinkle with cinnamon.

Yield: 4 to 6 servings.

Elderberry-Apple Relish

 A different and delicious treat to share with friends in their Christmas basket.

3 cups elderberries, washed and stemmed

3 cups green apples, pared and coarsely chopped

1 large onion, finely chopped

1 cup raisins

1 teaspoon ground ginger

¼ teaspoon cayenne pepper

1 teaspoon salt

1 teaspoon mustard seed

¼ teaspoon allspice

¾ cup brown sugar

1½ cups cider vinegar

Crush the berries slightly and place them in a large Dutch oven. Stir in the chopped apples, onion, and raisins. Add the remaining ingredients and bring to a boil over moderately high heat. Cook, stirring frequently, until mixture is thick. Ladle the hot relish into hot, sterilized jars and adjust lids.

Yield: 4 to 5 half-pints.

Spiced Elderberry Jam

This is an old recipe that goes back to Grandmother's day.

2 quarts elderberries, washed and stemmed	3 tablespoons lemon juice
6 cups sugar	½ teaspoon cinnamon
	¼ teaspoon ground cloves

Combine berries, sugar, lemon juice, and spices in a large Dutch oven. Stir to mix, lightly crushing some of the fruit. Over moderately high heat, bring the mixture to a boil. Cook rapidly until mixture is thick. Stir frequently to prevent sticking. When thick, stir and skim foam for 5 to 10 minutes. Ladle the hot jam into hot, sterilized jars and seal with melted paraffin.

Yield: 6 half-pints.

Elderblossom Wine

Pick only the blossom, leaving the bitter, fleshy stalks on the bush. Like berries, the blossoms should be picked only after the dew has been dried by the sun.

2 pounds sugar
1 gallon boiling water
3 cups elderberry
   blossoms, stemmed
juice of 1 lemon

½ cup medium-
   strength tea
1 package dry wine
   yeast

Combine the sugar with boiling water. Stir to dissolve sugar. Place elderberry blossoms in a clean 2-gallon crock and pour sugar mixture over flowers. When cool, stir in lemon juice, tea, and wine yeast. Cover the crock with plastic wrap and store at room temperature in a dark place for 5 days, pressing down surface foam twice daily. Siphon the liquid into a clean 1-gallon jug on the sixth day, leaving a 4-inch head space. Attach water lock and allow to stand at room temperature for 2 to 4 weeks, or until fermentation stops. Siphon wine into a clean 1-gallon jug, filling to the top, and store at 55°F. Siphon twice more, at 3-month intervals. Bottle wine at the end of the ninth month. Allow wine to mature 3 to 6 months before serving.

Yield: 1 gallon.

While driving through a park one summer afternoon, we recognized some blackcap bushes growing at the rear of a small maintenance building. With pails in hand and thoughts of warm raspberry pie on everyone's mind, we approached the thicket. The berries were large and plentiful so the childish chatter soon gave way to the plunking sound of berries dropping into buckets. Following the curve of the wild bushes, we soon found ourselves in a large grassy circle—entirely rimmed with wild raspberry canes! In the center of this area—as if by design—stood a magnificent, perfectly shaped tree offering shade from the hot sun. When the pails were mounded high with fruit and our fingers stained with sweet purple juice, we walked across the peaceful glen—stopping to admire the single majestic tree. That tree, which we had looked at and sat under, was ripe with black mulberries! Promising ourselves a return trip with empty pails the next afternoon, we admitted that our narrow view was a perfect example of not seeing the berries for the tree!

It seems fitting that such a beautiful tree as the mulberry, known since Greek-Roman times, should be the object of an impressive collection of fact and fable. The white mulberry tree—named for the color of its fruit—was cultivated in China for thousands of years for the feeding of silkworms. James I of England, apparently unaware of the silkworms' preference for the white mulberry, introduced the black species to his country in a futile attempt to create a new industry. A similar effort to promote a silk industry in the United States in 1820 failed disastrously because the white variety could not endure the harsh weather.

Pyramus and Thisbe, the ancient Babylonian counterparts of Romeo and Juliet, used the shade of a white mulberry tree outside the city gates as a secret trysting place when parted by their parents. Thisbe, arriving at the tree early one day, was frightened into a cave by a bloodied lion fresh from plundering a sheepfold. When Pyramus arrived, expecting to meet his lover, he found instead her veil—torn and red with blood. Imagining Thisbe slain, he plunged his sword through his heart. When sure the lion had passed, Thisbe ventured from hiding to approach the tree. There lay Pyramus with death clouding his eyes! Striking the blade into her own heart, she exclaimed:

> You tree, bear witness to the wrongs our parents have done to us. Let your berries be stained with our blood in token of their misdoing.

The hanging berries were splattered with the young girl's blood and supposedly still bear witness to the tragedy of the lovers.

The early European superstition that the devil blacked his boots with the berries did not seem to influence John Milton, whose mulberry tree at Cambridge is said to still bear fruit. Shakespeare's tree—planted in his Stratford garden—did not fare as well as Milton's. The man who bought Shakespeare's property, annoyed by the many people asking to see the tree, cut it down!

The three varieties of mulberry—red, white, and black—are elongated fruits composed of many drupelets. Growing from three-quarters of an inch to an inch and a half long, the berries can be eaten fresh or used for jams and pies. Closely resembling blackberries, the juicy berries have a sweet-tart flavor. The black mulberry—unlike its white relative—is resistant to cold climates and grows in Canada and the northern regions of the United States.

Mulberry-Rhubarb Pie

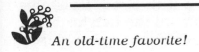

An old-time favorite!

2 cups mulberries,
  washed and picked
  over
1½ cups rhubarb,
  sliced
1 cup sugar

½ teaspoon nutmeg
¼ cup flour
  pastry for 9-inch, 2-
  crust pie
2 tablespoons butter

Preheat oven to 425°F.

Combine mulberries and sliced rhubarb in a medium bowl. In a small bowl combine sugar, nutmeg, and flour. Add sugar mixture to berries and rhubarb and stir lightly to mix. Spoon fruit mixture into pastry-lined 9-inch pie plate. Dot fruit with butter and cover with top crust. Seal the edges and cut steam vents. Bake in a preheated 425°F oven for 40 to 50 minutes, or until crust is golden and juices bubble.

Yield: 6 to 8 servings.

Mulberry-Apple Jelly

Because mulberries are low in pectin, they need some help in the jelling process. You can use liquid pectin as in other jelly recipes, or combine with apples, which add a nice flavor.

4– 5 cups mulberries
2 tart cooking apples, finely chopped

½ cup water
3–4 cups sugar

Combine the mulberries, chopped apples, and water in a medium saucepan and bring to a boil over moderate heat. Cover and reduce heat. Gently simmer the fruit for 20 to 25 minutes, or until soft. Strain the fruit through a jelly bag. Measure the juice and pour into a large Dutch oven. For every 2½ cups juice, add 2 cups sugar. Stir over moderate heat until sugar is dissolved. Increase heat slightly and bring mixture to a boil. Continue boiling for 10 to 15 minutes, or until a dab of jelly sets when placed on a cold plate. Stir and skim for 5 minutes. Pour jelly into hot, sterilized jars, leaving a ½-inch head space. Seat at once with melted paraffin.

Yield: 6 to 7 half-pints.

BUFFALO BERRIES

These acid-tasting orange or red berries are generally found growing in well-drained soil between Alaska and California. The bush—three to ten feet in height—has a smooth green oval leaf and produces clusters of tiny yellowish flowers in early spring.

The shiny, pearl-sized berries—too bitter to eat raw—probably received their name from the Indian practice of cooking them with buffalo meat. Containing a great deal of juice, the fruit can be cooked into a tart jelly or dried and sweetened to be used like currants.

THIMBLEBERRIES

This member of the rose family is often seen growing along the roadside in the upper reaches of the North American continent. The large pinkish white blossoms are easily mistaken for a variety of wild rose in June, but then give way to soft red berries that look very much like raspberries. The maple-shaped leaves are supported by thornless branches that provide easy picking.

We have frequently found these slightly dry tasting berries growing in and near patches of blackcaps and have added them to the harvesting pails. They combine well with other berries in pies and breads or can be used in the same manner as raspberries and blackberries.

These and many other berries can be found and used to enhance your daily menu planning. It only requires observation on the part of the harvester to locate the fruit and a little research to know if they are edible.

Summer is a joyful, generous season when Nature offers the comfort of warm days, blue skies, and abundant fresh food. It is a peaceful, reassuring season that beckons you to come outside, explore a dusty path, and sit under a tree. Come, savor the sights, sounds, and smells that have been enjoyed throughout the ages as you discover Cooking With Berries.

Bibliography

Anderson, Stanley F., with Hull, Raymond. *The Art of Making Wine.* New York: Hawthorn Books, 1970.

Bianchini, Francesco, and Corbetta, Francesco. *The Complete Book of Fruits and Vegetables.* New York: Crown Publishers, 1975.

Hardwick, Homer. *Winemaking at Home.* New York: Cornerstone Library, 1972.

Harrison, S. G.; Masefield, G. B.; and Wallis, Michael. *The Oxford Book of Food Plants.* London: Oxford University Press, 1969.

Huss, Tim. "The Cranberry Bogs of Long Island." *The Conservationist* (November–December, 1977): 5–8.

Hyams, Edward. *Plants in the Service of Man.* Philadelphia: J. B. Lippincott Co., 1971.

Medsger, Oliver Perry. *Edible Wild Plants.* New York: Collier Books, 1976.

Skinner, Charles M. *Myths and Legends of Flowers, Trees, Fruits, and Plants.* Philadelphia: J. B. Lippincott Co., 1911.

Turner, B. C. A. *Easy Guide to Home-made Wine.* Toronto-London: Mills and Boon, 1972.

Index